Life After Grief

A Soul Journey After Suicide

Jack Clarke

Personal Pathways Press

Life After Grief - A Soul Journey After Suicide

First Edition / July 1989

Publisher's Cataloging-in-Publication Data.

Clarke, Jack.

  Life After Grief.

  Bibliography.

  1. Grief.   2. Loss (Psychology).   3. Death.

4. Self-actualization.   5. Metaphysics   I. Title.

BF575C53   1989   88-090968

ISBN 0-929841-02-6

89 90 91 92 PPP 10 9 8 7 6 5 4 3 2 1

To Brenda, whose leaving

forced me to learn and grow again.

Table of Contents

Introduction

Jack Clarke's writing reflects a journey of profound spiritual growth and insight. From the suicide of his wife, through the grueling process of grief and mourning, to a spirit transformed by healing, Jack's work provides hope for the bereaved.

Life After Grief guides the reader through one man's poignant experience of grief and survival with honesty. The courage of this gentle, compassionate man is evident as his insights unfold. The reader is compelled to read on, to experience the feelings, the passions, the vulnerability and the hope.

Jack's story is the revelation of a man's personal odyssey of transformation, from suffering to spiritual awakening. His soul journey is told with clarity of focus, sharing success and failure. Powerful emotions, relationship struggles, a search for meaning and the risk of self examination highlight his work.

The deep psychic wound he received when his wife completed suicide led him to explore and accept ownership of his feelings for the first time in his life. He chose to reach out to a supportive network of friends and resources, and to deal honestly with his own previously masked codependency issues.

Jack's history, his vivid examination of his relationships and his willingness to explore the potentiality of the unknown, led him into an acceptance of new thought in psychology, metaphysics, and spirituality. He has maintained a balance between his interest in the higher-conscious self and the realism of an every-day-world of pain and suffering. He can now face his own eventual death, while at the same time he is learning, as he says, "to play with joy."

As a survivor of my own twenty-year-old son's suicide in 1977, it has been my privilege to walk part of this journey with Jack. I sat with him in 1984, at

i

his first Survivors of Suicide support group at The Link Counseling Center in Atlanta, Georgia. I felt his agony, his hopelessness, his annihilation. I experienced his compassion for others suffering a similar loss. I shared his tears.

Over the months and years since his wife's death, I also saw in Jack a will to live, to go beyond the existence of mere survival. I saw a man who wanted to find peace and harmony and meaning in his own life once again. Jack's writing was his vehicle for expression, an outpouring of emotions both terrible and wonderful. And now in its final form, his words in <u>Life After Grief</u> bring a sharing of great depth, understanding and comfort.

Jack is an inspiration to others as he tells of his battle with his own demons, his fears, his triumphs and his decision to continue to learn from his failures. His willingness to risk vulnerability with his readers stands as a role model for men and women to emulate. His search for healing and meaning continues to unfold, perhaps because he was willing to plunge into the eye of the hurricane rather than avoiding the tumultuous truth.

The bitter-sweet taste of this kind of honesty is indeed a gift of mixed blessings. He did not seek this kind of enlightenment, nor was it demanded of him. He slowly and deliberately chose to go through what might seem a crucifixion. He is surviving gloriously, a resurrection indeed!

> His pathway has been perilous,
> The price too high to pay,
> His footsteps have been charted;
> He found his chosen way...

Iris Bolton
Executive Director
The Link Counseling
Center

Preface

I wrote this book for several reasons. Foremost was my need to say farewell to the woman I loved for 13 years. We shared those years together as best we could with what we knew at the time.

Second, the book may give some comfort and hope to the hundreds of thousands of us whose lives have been permanently altered by a loved one's suicide. The lessons I learned after my wife died have gone a long way toward easing my grief and increasing my understanding of what happened.

There is very little literature available for coping with another's deliberate death, which is often the highest stress we will endure. I hope this book will help those who live on through dark days by serving as an example that learning and growth can come from tragedy.

Third, the book is my way of thanking the legions of friends, family and professionals who eased my pain. Though too numerous to be singled out, the results of their love and caring are woven throughout the book (names of some friends have been changed to protect their privacy). Without their beautiful insight and support, my joy today could not be.

Fourth, the book offers techniques for learning about the past, developed from my own experience. I believe past associations and events contribute to present dilemmas, and knowing more about that past helped me resolve some of my problems.

Fifth, I hope those who read the book come to believe, as I did, more strongly in life after death and a power even greater than our very important selves. I no longer fear death, though I want to live and learn as much as possible this time around.

Sixth, I hope the people, particularly men, who read this book can permit themselves to feel. We are in charge of our lives, and we can choose to feel if we want to. The pain is as intense with men as with women, but society prefers a stiff upper lip from men. Expressing our emotions may prolong our lives, since I am convinced that unexpressed emotions are killing people daily.

Seventh, those of you who share my codependent addiction to relationships may find some words of encouragement, since I have learned from several failed relationships. I chose women who didn't bring out the best in me and clung too tightly to those I became involved with. I too often tried to fix people rather than experiencing them for who they were. I hope you learn something from my struggle to find loving intimacy.

The path I have chosen is not for everyone, but it is a pilgrimage worth sharing. That journey has taken many twists and turns, but it has always led to my growth. My heart goes out to you on your own soul journey, whatever direction it takes. May you discover the wonderful person within you who is loving, supportive, and the best friend you'll ever have. And may the God around and within you strengthen you along your own path.

Jack Clarke
Marietta, Georgia
June, 1989

Chapter 1

Heartshock

July, 1984

I lost the center of my life on Friday, July 13, 1984 at 8:59 PM, a few minutes before the moon was at its fullest.

The night before, my wife and I had played a game of Trivial Pursuit at our neighbors' house. Dick and I played as a team against his wife Gini, Marguerite (another neighbor, whose husband Harry worked at night), and my wife Brenda. It was a rare occasion for me because Brenda disliked games for fun, perhaps because she was so preoccupied with her problems that she couldn't relax. The ladies nearly won a close match as we all enjoyed an Algerian red wine and each other's company. On the way home I noticed the moon looked full (a time when violent crimes increase) but didn't think much of it.

The next morning Brenda and I both awoke a bit groggy from the wine. I had business to attend to that morning, and I offered to stop by the grocery store on my way home, as Brenda looked unusually pale. She gladly accepted, for that afternoon she had an appointment with a new psychiatrist. She hoped to begin electroshock therapy, which we thought might relieve her manic depression. I assumed she was saving her strength for the ordeal of that first interview.

That afternoon, when I came home with the groceries, she was dressed and putting on her makeup. I asked if she wanted me to go with her to the interview, and she accepted. But I wasn't very enthusiastic, since we had consulted so many doctors together over the years for her extensive physical and psychological problems. None of them had seemed to help her very much.

She suffered from digestive problems, multiple allergies, painfully dry skin, hypoglycemia, psoriasis, arthritis, pre-menstrual syndrome (PMS), alcoholism and prescription drug abuse, a very low self-esteem, and, most devastating of all, manic depression. That year, at age 36, she had also begun the hot and cold flashes symptomatic of menopause, which had happened to her mother at about the same age.

The new doctor that day could not help. He and I failed to notice a signal of her depression, the black blouse she was wearing. He told her she didn't seem depressed, though she said she was, and he suggested she return when she was <u>really</u> depressed. He declined to consider electroshock therapy for her right away, instead recommending she see another doctor in his clinic who was working with experimental drugs.

2

Unfortunately, I didn't recognize his insensitivity and thought he knew what he was talking about.

Over a Chinese dinner that night she tearfully told me that she didn't want doctors poking her and sticking needles in her anymore. She didn't eat much of her meal, which was sweet and sour pork, normally her favorite. She was restless and asked if we could leave as soon as possible, which we did.

When we arrived home, she rushed to fix a strong bourbon and water, her normal drink, and went to sit on our front porch swing. After a few minutes, I went outside to see if she wanted to go to the Alcoholics Anonymous (AA) meeting that night while I attended the Al-Anon meeting, which supports families and friends of alcoholics. She said no, she was tired and would see me later.

I felt apprehensive and guilty about leaving her, but I experienced some peace of mind at Al-Anon and I felt I needed to go. My hunch said to stay, but my logic and my own need won out, so off I went. I'll never forget the little wave and tired smile she gave me from the front porch swing as I drove away from our house.

At the Al-Anon meeting I again gained much information that I could use regarding my life with an addictive person. At the close of the meeting, we linked hands and said the Lord's Prayer. It was around 9 PM, and I remember feeling particularly sad and anxious during the prayer. After talking with friends for a few minutes after the meeting, I drove home, arriving about 9:25 PM.

As I turned into the driveway, the sad feeling that had lingered since the prayer became ominously strong. The bright light was on in Brenda's bedroom, which was very unusual. I raced through the back door, seeing a long note in her writing on my nearby desk. After glancing at a few of her farewell words, I bolted for the stairs, passing the still playing television I had left on earlier. Taped to the bedroom door were additional notes with last minute thoughts of love and instructions for handling details.

With a mix of emotions impossible to describe, I approached the closed door, thinking that once again I'd have to get her to a hospital. She had attempted to kill herself three times before, taking overdoses of alcohol and pills.

She lay on the bed, face to the sky, eyes open, freed finally from a body and a life she did not like. She had broken her promise and used a bullet to deliver herself from her painful world to a hoped-for world without pain.

Over my objections, she had bought the gun two years earlier for protection on a trip alone to Florida. I had thought on many occasions I should get rid of it, because of her suicidal tendencies. However, she had said emphatically that if she ever killed herself, she would not use a gun, so her relatives could view her body. Several weeks before, a strong urge came over me to at least hide the gun, but she could become very angry when I disturbed her possessions, so I left it in her closet.

A red stain covered the wall behind her head. I walked over closer, but couldn't touch her. I knew she was gone from this life as I began slipping into the shock that would last many months. Before the shock set in to shield me from my sense of desperation, failure, and loss, though, an urgency to get help quickly spurred me into action.

I remembered seeing Dick, Gini, and Marguerite walking up the street as I drove in. I don't think they had moved fifteen steps since then as time seemed to stand still. I ran into the street with my arms waving in the air, shouting that Brenda had killed herself. They couldn't believe what I was saying but I begged them to please help me. Dick then made what he later told me was the most difficult phone call of his life, summoning the police. Before they arrived, I cried hard for the first of many times, leaning against Dick's car in their carport. I didn't want to believe she was gone, but knew she was.

After awhile, my neighbors took me inside to make the necessary terrible phone calls. With Dick's help, I first called Brenda's brother so he could make arrangements to tell Brenda's mother, who lived nearby. I next called her twin sister, Glenda, and her husband Fred (who lived in Virginia) and then my mother. Overwhelming feelings of failure and unbearable sadness gripped me as I made the calls. The pain for me really began with those horror filled minutes on the phone with loved ones.

It seemed forever until the fire truck arrived. I wondered "Why a fire truck?," but remembered firemen are often trained paramedics. The police arrived later and seemed to take an eternity investigating the scene while I sat staring blankly toward nowhere in Dick and Gini's den. When the police finally came over to talk to me, I asked if there was any chance Brenda could have been saved. They looked compassionate as they shook their heads sadly, saying "No." The hearse came to take Brenda's body away.

My mother offered to let me stay at her house, but I decided to remain at Dick and Gini's. I was in no condition to do anything that night, particularly drive. Dick, Gini, Harry and Marguerite, bravely crossed the street to clean up Brenda's room. I can't imagine how they had the courage to do so, since they all loved her and were in shock themselves.

Words came to me over and over again that sleepless night. They were "All you can do is learn and grow from this." I had no idea how I was going to learn and grow without the love of my life. I believe those words of encouragement came from some power higher than my conscious mind, for all I could consciously think about was that Brenda was gone and I had failed to keep her alive.

I learned later that most suicides don't leave a note, and those that do often leave bitter ones. Brenda's detailed notes inspired her loved ones and friends, helping us cope in the dark days that followed. She signed the long note "S.W.," which was her favorite of the many nicknames I had for her. It was short for "Sweetie," which became "S.W. Eetie." In her final hour she added several notes on small pieces of paper, as she thought of other people she had forgotten. Here are the actual notes, as she left them for us (I have added some comments in parentheses for clarification):

One note was taped to my door, written in large letters on her business stationery:

Jack - instructions on your desk -
I love you but I'm tired -

On my desk, written on paper torn out of a notebook, was her main note:

Forgive the scratchy writing - I'm in a hurry -
7/13/84

1. Mother - I love you & if you go to pieces over this I'll be watching you from heaven & I'll be ashamed of you. Get out, enjoy life and do something useful --- you have so much laughter &

joy to spread & you're <u>so young</u>. I know God will find something great for me to do helping others. I've got a talent for that & I'm sure he'll forgive me for what I'm doing.

      2. *Jack - I'm nothing but a big expense - I don't think I can take being a mill-stone anymore - I love you - you've been so good to me - but you deserve more happiness. Thank you, for taking care of Jay* (her son) *& I, but don't grieve for me - God will give me a job & I'll be happy & won't be depressed. Please let my family choose if they want to see me privately before I'm cremated & then have a memorial service 2 days after. With Rev. Wix* (the Baptist minister who had married us) *if possible - invite all my friends & then have some back to drink a glass of champagne to my success at my next job. Please have Ed* (Wix) *do "Crossing the Bar" & some more of his lovely poems & tell Ed how much I love him. The main thing I request is - find someone new - I'd like you & Julia* (my first wife) *to get back together - now you have so much in common. You can raise her child & you'll be a much better husband. I've always liked her ---*
      Do not grieve over me - I don't belong here.

      Sherrie (her best friend)- *I love you - I think you know what your order was & can figure it out.*

I want you to have all of my clothes & jewelry that I don't leave to my sister & any of my pictures on my bedroom walls that Jack may want to part with some day. You have been my fortress thru many storms & I'll be watching you so be good.

Glenda (her identical twin sister) - *I would like you to have my jewelry - Bobby's* (her high school friend) *ring because he was all of our friends. Anything that Jack doesn't want for sentimental reasons and all of my shoes. All my clothes but let Sherrie have the ones that fit her and some of the jewelry - she has none. If Jack will part with my precious rings - I'd like for Sherrie to have my present wedding set & you my one with the 8 precious stones. - That's Jack's decision. You & Sherrie get together & decide & ask Jack --*

Jay - *I have always loved you - I'm proud of you - I tried to call you tonight - I even called Mr. Lawrence & Mr. Day* (her son's probation officers in California). *I'm sorry I didn't get to see you, but I'm proud of what you've accomplished & I'm going to be up in heaven watching over you. It's been a rough road for us both. I'm sorry to say I wasn't together enough myself to be of much help to you but will you do me a favor & try to carry on what I couldn't do for you. I have had this severe depression problem since age 10 - so you had*

9

nothing to do with it. I'm going on to try to see if God will give me a job helping others not to have the same trouble. I do love you. MOTHER

Don't have music or flowers at my memorial - send donations to the Lupus Foundation or the Arthritis Foundation.

And No Sadness. And everybody remember - I was fun to be around & carry on the tradition.

I'm going to a better place & I'm sure God will forgive me for what I'm doing - I don't see any other choice and he may have a better choice for me.

Jack - even if this is messy, would you please copy sections for any of the people I've mentioned. I tried to tape it but couldn't find any tapes for the little recorder.

Jack - I do love you. I'm sorry I've been so much trouble & expense but - don't let this get you down - I have a job to do & I know it isn't on this earth - it's up in heaven guiding others. So don't get too upset over this,

Please - **GET ON WITH YOUR LIFE**

Love,

S.W.

P.S. I'll be watching
you so don't screw up!

Taped to her door, written on a piece of note-paper from her small bedroom desk, some afterthought messages to other friends:

To - Barbara Stelling
I love you & I'm sorry
I couldn't discuss this
with you - it came up
suddenly & I couldn't
explain - I'm so proud
of you! Keep up the good
work & be happy!

To: Linda Blackstone
& Sue - I've tried
calling a couple of times
just to say hi - but I
do love you.

To Gini & Marguerite
Good neighbors - Good friends
I love you & Dick & Harry, too.

On her bedstand, on the same notepaper, with bloodstains on it, was:

*Time of
Death?*

*Shot myself at
approximately 8:59*

Her notes gave all of us the strength to carry on as the days, weeks, and months slowly trudged along. The notes were the last of many kind acts she had performed over her lifetime, in spite of her addictions and afflictions. Those maladies often made it hell to live with her; now my hell was to live without her.

I was determined to go on with a life that had little meaning for me then. Her pain was over, mine was just beginning. I couldn't possibly foresee the depths of depression nor the pinnacles of new discoveries I was to make. I was cast adrift by the one I loved, embarking on a journey I did not want, but had to make.

Why couldn't she cope with this life? Why did she leave me? Why did this tragedy have to happen? Why me? Why? Why?

Chapter 2

Why Me?

December, 1940 - July, 1971

Why had this happened to me? Where had I gone wrong? What had I done to deserve such pain? Was I different from everyone else? To better understand what I learned after Brenda's death, it may help to know some of my background.

I'm about as typical white American male as you can get. I stand a shade over six feet tall, stay fairly thin (170 pounds), have brown receding hair (with quite a bit of white in what's left), and I'm physically healthy with often overly sensitive emotions. I've been told I resemble the comedian Bob Hope or the actor Larry Hagman, though I hope I don't act like his most famous character, J. R. on the TV show "Dallas."

I came into this world on December 28, 1940, about 7:50 PM in a suburban hospital near New York City. My parents and I lived in a comfortable house, though I remember most the sandbox and the huge chestnut tree behind the house. I loved digging in the sand and wondering how a tree could be so huge.

My father was in his mid-forties when I was born, so as I grew older he was more like a grandfather in many ways. My mother's mother was the only grandparent alive when I was born. Mom was in her mid-twenties, a transplanted Southern belle who had met my father in New York after his first marriage ended in divorce.

Both worked hard building my father's food service equipment business during my early years, often leaving me in the care of a wonderful black man or my jovial aunt, who was a devout Christian Science healer. I loved them both, finding them easier to take advantage of than my strict parents.

In 1943, my brother Penn came into the world. He became my playmate and often my responsibility. Two years after he was born I was off to kindergarten with an already developed love of reading and a painful shyness that would continue for years. Though the school bullies found me an easy target, I was a very fast runner, leaving them behind most of the time.

After a mean first grade teacher, my second grade teacher was too lenient, fostering in me a lazy tendency. Fortunately, in third grade Mrs. Flynn changed that. She was very tough on me, forcing me to finish my work and do it well. I now realize she reinforced (with my parents) my love of reading and a work discipline.

I learned faster than most of my classmates, which for many years gave me a feeling of superiority. I needed that feeling, since I believe my childhood experiences ingrained in me a low self-esteem that still challenges me. I also stayed pretty much to myself, indulging in wild imaginary worlds that would later lead me into reading every science fiction book I could find. Those early days did not include formal religious training, though my aunt and my strict, moral parents were certainly a spiritual influence.

My surroundings and safe environment changed in 1950 when my father sold his business to a company outside Chicago. We moved to suburban Evanston so he could continue to run the food service equipment division into which his company had been merged. I had only one close friend in New York, so the move wasn't as traumatic as it might have been. The major change for me was downscaling from a large comfortable house with yard all around it to a small third-story two-bedroom apartment.

A year or so after moving, my aunt died back in New York. Because I didn't attend the funeral, her passing was never real to me. At that time, I was much more interested in collecting baseball cards and reading, anyway. She would be the only close family member that died for nearly 30 years.

My parents decided it was time for Penn and me to have some exposure to formal religion at a church in Evanston. Though we were taught Christian principles at home, we had never attended a church regularly. They thought their sons should have an opportunity to decide for ourselves if organized religion appealed to us. Therefore, we began attending a Presbyterian church in town.

My brother and I went with fluctuating frequency for several years. Somehow, the interpretations I heard about the Bible didn't always feel quite accurate to me. I've not particularly attracted to ritual, either. I can't really say those times at church were good or bad; perhaps the word indifferent would best describe my feelings.

I liked my new grade school, and the neighborhood we lived in had plenty of playmates. Being small for my age and quiet by nature, I really only had one close friend, Bill, who was also small. We talked and played together often, since he lived only two blocks away.

Grade school ended and junior high began, where once again I had to meet and get along with new people. Bill and I were in the same homeroom and members of the same YMCA club. Neither of us had developed an interest in girls yet, unlike most of our classmates, who were not as shy as we were.

Around that time, my parents bought a lot on a lake outside Chicago, and we all pitched in to help build our vacation lake house. When finished, we spent many weekends and most of our summers there. Penn and I learned to drive a boat, water ski and ice skate, all of which helped build my often shaky confidence.

My early high school years frustrated me. I began to have an interest in dating, but my small size and quiet nature did not appeal to the cheerleaders I expected to date. I also developed a love for football, finding that I could catch well and run fast. My short stature worked against me again, though, so I had to be content acting as a manager for the high school football team.

Because of my ability to learn quickly, I was placed in honors and college level courses, forcing me to work hard for top grades. I had dreams of attending an Ivy League school to become an engineer. My mother enrolled me in ballroom dancing classes, where my first crush wouldn't acknowledge my existence. In short, I resembled the classic "nerd" for my first three years of high school.

Finally, late in my junior year, I began to grow taller. I dated younger girls, since my own class remembered me as I had been. No real romance yet, though. My confidence grew also, for I ran for class president my senior year, though I lost to a friend of mine. He was headed for Yale, and so was I, I thought.

But that wasn't to be. Though in the top 12 percent of my class at one of the finest high schools in the country at Evanston, Yale (and MIT and Princeton) wanted those who finished in the first 10 percent. I was accepted at Cornell and looked forward to my Ivy League life.

My last six weeks of high school were great fun. My parents had moved permanently to the lake house, so I stayed with a friend in Evanston until graduation. What my folks didn't know was that his parents were in India, so those last weeks were one big party. I had my first beer then. It tasted awful, but I wanted to be one of the guys. I would spend a great deal of my life going along with the crowd.

My freshman year in mechanical engineering at Cornell was fine academically, but frustrating socially. I missed the friendlier atmosphere of the Midwest, so my sophomore year I transferred to the University of Wisconsin at Madison, which was only 70 miles from our lake house.

My years at Wisconsin were filled with fraternity life, leadership positions and fine education. I worked during the summers and at the fraternity to pay for about a third of my education costs.

The first two years there, I tried to set dating records in my effort to make up for lost time with women. I seemed to have a different date every night of every weekend, never giving a relationship time to develop. In retrospect, I didn't have a steady girl friend throughout my teenage years.

The third year, 1962, brought my first real relationship, a new college major and a move of our home. The relationship lasted for several months that spring when I was president of my fraternity, culminating in our being pinned. Unfortunately, over the summer, she grew infatuated with my fraternity vice president and chose to be pinned to him instead. This was my first real heartbreak, though a part of me was glad to be dating freely again.

To the displeasure of my parents, I decided to switch from engineering to the business school because thermodynamics and fluid mechanics failed to interest me. I wanted to be a salesman in a technical field, like my father. I felt I had enough technical background already and wanted more business training.

That year, my father left his corporate job and my parents moved to Atlanta, my mother's hometown. We had visited Atlanta nearly every year of my life to stay with my grandmother. I loved my times spent there, so I felt good about the move, though I would miss the lake house and would have long drives back and forth between school and home.

My senior year I was again elected fraternity president and experienced my second real relationship. She was president of her sorority, so we had much to talk about, including our infatuation with each other. I wasn't very aggressive with her, or anyone else I dated, thus remaining a virgin throughout college.

After I graduated, she and some friends of hers met my brother and me in Rome, Italy. We were touring Europe on only six dollars a day, having taken a multiple-stop budget air trip, eating cheaply, and often staying in youth hostels. That seven-week trip was a wonderful relief for me, for I faced an ROTC mandated two-year tour in the Army when we returned.

The rendezvous in Rome was a real highlight of my life to that point, a true rite of passage for me. For the first time, I spent the night with a woman. She and that night remain very special memories. We parted after Rome and have led separate lives since then.

Arriving home (wearing longer hair and a rebellious mustache), I was lucky enough to be stationed with the Army in Atlanta after basic training. That allowed me to live at home with my parents and commute to Fort McPherson. Since I was an Infantry officer and Vietnam was heating up, I did a first-rate job with the Recruiting Service assignment. I wasn't interested in jungle warfare or being a hero.

I also met and dated for many months a lovely Southern belle. She helped me forget my college sweetheart and endure my first few months in the Army. She wanted more commitment than I was willing to give, so we stopped seeing each other soon after I returned to Atlanta and Fort McPherson.

The two service years became a blur of Army travel and party weekends. I began to date debutantes, thanks to some of my mother's family connections. The process was simple, as they normally called me for a date, or we were paired together by those who ran the parties. Also during that time I often escorted my mother and grandmother to the opera, where I learned a great deal from them about music.

The Army days came to an end, and my computer sales career began with Honeywell. My plan to sell in a technical field succeeded as I enjoyed the heady early times of the computer revolution. The debutante parties continued, filling nights and weekends, so no real female relationship of any depth developed, because I had decided to continue playing the field.

In retrospect, those college, Army, and early computer sales years were one long vacation from thinking or feeling. Life was just one big party to me, with work a necessary requirement to produce what little spending money I needed.

My parents charged me only a nominal amount to live with them. We had a garage apartment that had been converted to a one room party place we called "The Outback," where my brother and I held numerous parties.

All that changed when I began dating Julia in 1966. Though she had been a debutante, I identified with her because she had rebelled against the society world. I had begun to have reservations about the shallowness of some of the parties, thoughts that were supported by her.

She wanted to be an artist or musician, and for the first time in years I began to think again as we spent hours talking and playing together during the

21

months we dated. I downplayed the seriousness of our relationship to my family and friends, so they were shocked when we announced suddenly we were planning to marry in two weeks.

My parents were furious that I had lied to them about the seriousness of our relationship. We had already picked out an apartment and decided we didn't want parties and the normal fuss of a society wedding. The ceremony at her parents' house found me crying, a very rare occurrence for me because I had learned the American tradition that men don't cry.

Julia and I set up housekeeping and began to adjust to living with each other. We socialized a lot, and enjoyed acting very childish most of the time, which was how we communicated. Friends grew tired of our constant baby talk, but we enjoyed acting more like children than adult husband and wife.

We didn't really communicate, choosing to suppress our feelings of love and anger, and never fought. We settled for an uneasy roommate relationship that became less and less comfortable as the 60's became the 70's. Our marriage continued to deteriorate as we moved once, and I left Honeywell for a sales job at Hewlett-Packard.

We decided to try some counseling. I believed we were in therapy to help her change, since I didn't think my behavior was part of our problem. My self concept didn't allow for me to have faults. These sessions introduced me to my passive aggressiveness, though it would be years before I recognized and dealt with this tendency to stuff my feelings (to get even rather than getting mad).

Counseling can't work under such conditions, and it didn't. Our only fight was vicious and physical as my suppressed rage finally surfaced. I remember her saying as I cried after the fight that she didn't think I cared that much. I did care, but could never express my emotions. Our four-year marriage was ended.

My background had not prepared me for sharing feelings, nor had I any concept of how to deal with severe loss. Two weeks before my amicable divorce was final, I met Brenda. That left virtually no time to grieve over the lost marriage.

Julia and I had married to get away from our parents' homes rather than for real love. Since we ended amicably, and there were no children, we remain friendly today. She and I have since talked often about our addictions.

The tendency to jump from one relationship to another, I would learn much later, is a classic symptom of an addictive behavior pattern called codependence. Basically, this term describes those of us who turn over responsibility for our own happiness to someone else.

Though I'll say more on this later, we become addicted to having someone in our lives so we can be happy. We also have a tendency to find addictive people we think we can fix. We have difficulty knowing what we want, or what we feel, because we spend most of our time trying to please and appease others.

But I didn't understand that then, and by then I had met Brenda.

Chapter 3

The Brenda Years

July, 1971 - July, 1984

Brenda was a very beautiful woman. Her dark brown hair set off equally dark brown eyes that were often the only window to her emotions. She never felt tall enough at 5' 4", nor did she consider herself well-endowed, but I thought she looked terrific most of the time.

She was bright and charming at times, but also complaining and lethargic more often than I liked. When she wasn't depressed she was always meticulously groomed, though she used more makeup than I thought she needed for her pretty skin. She seemed to hide behind the makeup, perhaps to mask her depression.

Not only was she beautiful physically, she was a truly caring person inside, though that compassion was sometimes masked by drugs, alcohol or her depressions. Most of her friends felt blessed by the friendship.

Even though she was often in emotional and physical pain, she was always there when friends needed her. She never forgot a birthday or anniversary and was always sending silly or encouraging cards. Whenever it was needed, she had the ability to provide comfort, love, or a proper scolding.

Her bubbly personality, beauty, and intelligence usually made her a center of attention at any gathering. Over the years, she had developed these qualities to such a point that, even though she was terribly depressed and desperate, no one could tell. She was a marvelous actress.

Over the years I became aware of how much energy the acting cost her. I often felt she gave her energy to friends, leaving little for me. Only after it was too late did her friends realize the price she paid for her show of enthusiasm. Most were unaware of her need to "put on a happy face" to cover her depression.

Brenda was born the first of identical twins outside Atlanta in Dallas, Georgia, at 9:45 AM, April 23rd, 1948. She had married her high school sweetheart at age 19 and they later had a son named Jay. As with many early marriages, this one failed.

I had not really noticed her around the office, perhaps because she had allowed her appearance to deteriorate as her four-year marriage ended. A mutual friend introduced us just prior to our individual divorces becoming final.

26

I wasn't in the best of spirits then. I had been trained to succeed, but my marriage of four years had also failed. I didn't realize it then, but we were both recovering and grieving from the loss of those marriages.

Brenda and I double dated with Penn. Brenda had regained her looks and figure, and I, at age 30, saw her as a beautiful 23-year-old brunette with long flowing hair and a good mind. She was not as entranced with me that night as I was with her, but I persuaded her to see me again. Thus began a never-boring three-year courtship.

No one in our office knew we were dating except our friend and my secretary, also a mutual friend. We had fun with this situation, calling each other "Joyce" and "Henry" in order to talk about the other around the office without anyone knowing. (It would be my secretary's compassionate policeman brother-in-law who came to our house thirteen years later to investigate Brenda's death.)

In late 1972, after a year of dating, I decided to take three weeks vacation and travel to Hawaii and Australia without her. I missed her terribly during that trip, particularly since I became fascinated with Australia and wanted to share my experiences in that extraordinary country with her. She told me later she hadn't expected me to come back. In truth, I might have stayed there if not for her.

I found the Aussies friendly, honest, and happy. I decided during the trip to leave my successful career selling computers to take over Penn's thriving Atlanta real estate business. He was headed out on another of his world trips and I was ready to take a business risk.

I worked hard selling real estate in 1973 and rewarded myself by taking a three-week trip with Brenda to Europe. She had not travelled much and was thrilled to go. Her mother Grace gladly looked after Jay, who was her eldest grandchild.

I was exhausted from overworking right up to the day we left, so the trip began with Brenda nursing me. I literally staggered onto the airplane. After resting in England, the trip became a wonderful experience as I watched her joy in discovering the world. We fell more deeply in love.

Brenda and I learned a great deal about each other during that trip. The stress of travel teaches much about the nature of people, and we found that, even though there were moments of strain, we enjoyed our experiences.

That Christmas, I gave her a ring, though not the "right one." She expected an engagement ring, not the dinner ring I gave her. Several days later she threw the ring across her office and our relationship faltered, to say the least.

Talk of marriage scared me because of my fear of failure. Freedom from personal commitment still appealed to me, too, so we decided to date other people in early 1974. However, we both found dating others tedious and unsatisfying, frequently telling one another about those dates afterwards.

Dating others turned out to be the catalyst needed, and, helped by advice from good friends, we decided to marry that August. My family accepted Brenda more than they had Julia. The wedding was held at my parents' house and my mother gave me one of her favorite rings to give to Brenda as an engagement ring.

My mother's generosity was helpful, because the real estate market had gone sour in Atlanta. Much of my earnings and savings had been invested in some of the raw land tracts I was selling in 1973 but couldn't resell in 1974. Thus, we married nearly broke, with only the money Brenda made for our income.

Once again, I cried so hard at the wedding that I could barely say the vows. Looking back, I don't know if they were tears of joy or some premonition of our future. I do remember that the day was one of mixed emotions for me, perhaps because I had never resolved losses from my first marriage.

The ceremony was taped and remains one of the few recordings I have of Brenda talking, along with some answering machine tapes. I wish Brenda could have found happiness in using her beautiful voice. She could sing harmony to a song the first time she heard it, perhaps because she sensed the music before it was actually heard. She, her sister Glenda, and their

29

friend Sherrie could harmonize together as well as any professional group.

After the ceremony, we drove to our new apartment and spent our honeymoon there. We both weren't interested in having a house and all the upkeep needed. Along with Jay, we settled into a fairly leisurely time at the apartment, where we lived for five years.

Her income couldn't support us so I returned to Hewlett-Packard to sell computers again. She was having trouble at work because of her codependent tendency to take personal responsibility for fixing other people's problems. She now worked for the Director of Nursing at a nearby hospital after leaving Hewlett-Packard before we were married. When that job became too difficult to handle she left and performed temporary work.

I could never understand why she wasn't able to cope with a job, nor why she couldn't develop a hobby or participate in volunteer work. My goal-directed, success-oriented background made it difficult for me to sympathize with Brenda's lack of work-related goals. I thought she just didn't have the willpower to do something with her life.

We just couldn't seem to communicate to each other our frustration and confusion. She started drinking more and taking increased amounts of prescription drugs from many doctors. We began to have fights, particularly in May of each year, and Jay began having trouble at school.

His father and stepmother had moved to California, and after much soul searching, all five of us agreed that he would try living with them. This allowed Brenda to travel with me on my business trips, which we both enjoyed. We never talked about nor showed any emotion over the loss of Jay to his father, perhaps in the mistaken belief that the problem would just go away if we ignored it.

Around that time, I was promoted to a sales manager's role, which increased my responsibilities and decreased my freedom, creating stress. My parents moved to a smaller, one level house to accommodate his failing health. His decline, and my mother's anxious reaction to that decline, added more stress to our lives.

Our fights increased dramatically as the various stresses on our lives took their toll. Brenda continued to be depressed for no obvious reason; I was unhappy with my boss; the real estate holdings which drained our checkbook didn't sell; Jay was not doing well in California; and I was headed towards my fortieth year, a time of high stress for most men. To top it off, we drank too much alcohol. However, I did play a great deal of tennis during that time period to work off some of my tension.

In retrospect, Brenda and I were grieving over the loss of Jay and having too little cash to pay the bills (another loss). I was mourning my loss of youth, my loss of freedom in my sales position, and my father's failing health. Our backgrounds didn't prepare us to deal with these multiple losses, so we ranted and raved at each other, often spurred on by lowered inhibitions from drinking.

To try to ease the pressure and change our way of living, I transferred to another division of Hewlett-Packard as a salesman again and we decided to move. We had chosen a fine new apartment near the Chatta-hoochee River in Atlanta when a friend at work suggested we look at a house in his neighborhood in the suburb of Marietta. We liked the house immediately, including its low price, so we bought it in September, 1979.

The house needed a lot of work, which we enjoyed doing together, much to our surprise. We felt a real sense of accomplishment as we saw the house improve with our efforts. But stress reappeared when Brenda fell down the steps while I was out of town a few weeks after we moved in. She injured her back in the fall, which began a nearly five-year odyssey to doctors, chiropractors, osteopaths, and massage therapists as she tried to correct the problem.

Even with improvements in my life, my internal pressure continued to build. One day I ended a business trip early and sought help on my own at several mental health offices. I hoped I'd find a counselor that could explain why I felt so uptight.

I was desperate, frustrated, angry and depressed, without really knowing why. I now believe I was near my own breaking point. Without the release of normal grief emotions over my cumulative losses, I was like an overfilled balloon drifting closer and closer to a porcupine.

No one that I called on could see me right away, until a kindly social worker at Ridgeview Institute sat down and talked to me. He convinced me that counseling might help. Emotionally exhausted, I drove home. I told Brenda I was going to begin counseling, and she agreed to do the same.

Unfortunately, the counseling didn't affect me much for a long time, because, as earlier with Julia, I continued to think there was nothing wrong with <u>me</u>. Also, though the counselors did the best they knew how, I honestly believe they couldn't help us.

They concentrated on my passive aggressive behavior, which I wouldn't acknowledge. It would take me years of reading books, talking to counselors, listening to Brenda and friends, and self-analysis before I realized I needed to change my behavior, too.

One of the counselors recommended Dr. Wayne Dyer's wonderful book <u>The Sky's The Limit</u>. The second chapter of that book finally convinced me that I, too, needed to change. It described many traits of the authoritarian personality that I didn't like in others, which I saw particularly in Brenda.

But the real revelation was that I, too, had some of those traits I so disliked in others. They were only "mirroring" my own tendencies. I finally paid attention to how I was behaving.

Authoritarians like to have everything neat and categorized, as I did. I was meticulous about adhering to rules, even in unimportant games. I also had to admit that I had difficulty seeing grey areas. I tended to classify people as all good or bad, rich or poor, right or wrong, etc. I was generally not open to new ways of thinking or other ways of looking at life. I conformed rather blindly to the standards and morals of my own white ethnic group. I couldn't understand weaknesses in others.

In February 1980, we travelled across town to a going away party for my secretary. She was moving to Florida, and I knew we would both miss her free-wheeling attitude. She tells it like it is and loves to party, both of which appealed to us. Brenda had gained a lot of weight since falling down the stairs, and felt threatened by the many attractive women at the party. We both drank too much, but managed to arrive home around 1 AM.

We had been sleeping in separate bedrooms. We said we did so because of her chronic insomnia and my tendency to snore, but I think now we were both frightened of true intimacy. I had retired to my room, but something kept me awake. I hadn't heard her door close. She had been running up and down the stairs, then went into her bathroom for a long time. I got up groggily and knocked on the door.

She screamed "Leave me ALONE!" I knew something was very wrong, so I ran downstairs to find a toothpick to jimmy the lock on her bathroom door. A glance at a note left on the kitchen table showed me that she was trying to kill herself and I ran upstairs.

I successfully opened the door, to see her swallowing handfuls of pills from her well-stocked medicine cabinet. I grabbed her and dragged her downstairs, holding tightly onto the clenched hand that still clutched some pills. She promised not to take them if I let her go, but she tried to do just that as soon as I released her.

I slapped her and she fell to the floor, hitting her head as pills scattered everywhere. In a tentative voice she said she was all right, so I then coaxed her back upstairs to her bed. Unfortunately, her conversation became more and more jumbled and vague.

I was as scared as I'd ever been in my life. I had the life of the one I loved in my hands. I had never been confronted by a life and death situation before. I was desperately afraid I would lose her. She was becoming less and less lucid every minute. But what should I do?

I called her counselor who talked with her, then advised me to get her to a hospital. I tried to lift her but couldn't, so I called the police for assistance. A considerate policeman responded quickly, without lights and siren, and helped me carry Brenda to my car. Since I had been drinking earlier, I asked him to follow me.

At the hospital, a medical team pumped her stomach but she lapsed into a coma. I thought at the time I could never feel as empty and desperate as I felt in that waiting room, but time would tell differently. Brenda's family and I waited two days for her to awaken from the coma. She was very surprised to be alive, though all of us were glad she was still with us.

She was then admitted to a psychiatric hospital. They diagnosed her as a manic-depressive and began lithium treatments, the only known control for her condition. Her mood swings were very fast, from manic hyper-activity to a hibernating form of depression when she wouldn't leave her bedroom for days. Until the doctors diagnosed these swings as manic-depression, I didn't know what the term meant.

Unfortunately lithium turned out to be one of Brenda's many allergic substances. Her white cell count skyrocketed, endangering her health, so after a few weeks of treatment, she was placed back on tranquilizers and taken off the lithium treatments.

She vowed never to return to such a hospital and she really tried to find a way to live. The next four years were our happiest as we learned more about ourselves and each other, worked on the house, and travelled together.

Since she didn't have a regular job, I was given the gift of her company on my business trips. I was glad she could travel with me, because I feared what might happen while I was away. On top of her other problems, she often had nightmares so realistic that twice she had called the police to say someone was in her room. When they arrived, they would find no one or any trace of anyone else in the second floor bedroom.

My father, who was a warm, positive, extraordinarily energetic man who often showed his emotions openly, died in August, 1980. His anger at times was intimidating, but he was a gregarious, positive man most of his life. His declining health in his eighties had been hard on my mother, opening a gap between Mom and me that widened after his death.

Perhaps I needed to protect and strengthen my fragile new behavior patterns, learned from books and counseling. For me the answer then was to run from my strong mother for awhile as I concentrated on my problems with Brenda. I didn't understand at that time that my mother was grieving after losing her husband of over 40 years, and I didn't want to acknowledge my own fear of losing Brenda to suicide.

I left Hewlett-Packard in 1981 to take the first of three computer sales and management jobs during the next two years. The emerging new me felt more able to cope in the business world without the protective umbrella of a large corporation.

I found some contentment and a strong sense of accomplishment working in our garden during this period. The house sits on nearly two thirds of an acre of land with excellent sandy loam soil on top of clay. Watching the hundreds of azaleas, roses, dogwoods, maples and other bushes I planted grow and bloom under my care was a source of real joy for me.

I looked forward to times spent in the garden much more than going to work or being with my family. Those hours spent digging, pruning, fertilizing, and watering helped me keep my balance in a world I found increasingly troublesome. Gardening kept me outdoors, where I was less inclined to dwell extensively on past problems and my worries about the future, which I now know is a codependent tendency.

I left the third computer job in October, 1983 to again try to sell our real estate holdings and to travel with Brenda to the South Seas. We were very excited about the trip, which would include a return to Australia for me.

Brenda's physical problems were further complicated when a drunk friend stumbled into and fell on top of her at our house after dinner a month later. The next day she was admitted to the hospital once more. She was bleeding internally from the reopening of a surgical wound from an operation she had undergone to correct an intestinal problem.

She was devastated when the man refused to acknowledge responsibility for injuring her. She believed that no matter what she tried, she would never be healthy. Her back still bothered her, the allergies remained, digestion was irregular, the drinking and pill-taking continued, and her recurring depression always loomed in front of her.

Brenda wanted the deed to our house changed to include spouse's right of survivorship language and our wills updated before the trip, which we did. These were clues to Brenda's return to suicidal thinking, but I didn't recognize them at the time.

A few days before we were to leave for the South Seas Brenda drank too much during a dinner with Sherrie and her husband Nick. She deliberately overdosed herself that night with pills and alcohol. This time I did not know what happened until I came home for lunch just as she wandered out of her room completely incoherent. Looking in her room I found a vague and rambling farewell note and a pocketful of assorted pills in her robe.

Luckily, she had gone to sleep before taking too many of the pills. A call to the counselor brought the suggestion that I walk her around and force coffee down her until she became coherent again. I was tired of saving her life, so I tape recorded her rambling conversation, hoping that if she could hear herself in such a state she would change somehow.

After a few hours she began to come around and I angrily played the tape for her. When it finished playing she apologized for the trouble she was causing me, but said she was just tired of fighting life.

When I asked if she still wanted to take the trip, she said "Yes." I hoped the summer weather "Down Under" plus the radical change of scenery and the happy Australian people would make a big difference in her will to live and in our attitude about each other.

That night we were scheduled to attend a rehearsal dinner for one of my cousins. Brenda didn't feel up to going with me and I didn't want to leave her, but my mother expected us at the dinner.

I didn't want to displease Mom by staying home with Brenda, so I made the excuse that she was sick. I worried throughout the dinner, torn between concern over Brenda and loyalty to Mom and family, wishing I was already on my way to the South Seas without all these problems.

The next week we did pack our bags, complete with her two special pillows - she felt she would sleep better with them - and left our house occupied by a neighbor's son who agreed to house sit for us. We were finally going on the trip I had dreamed about for 12 years.

We loved Australia. The sunny climate and even sunnier disposition of the Aussies was a tonic for both of us. Her insomnia sometimes caused us to hop from one hotel to another, but that didn't stop the two month trip from being wonderful. She took notes on the colorful words used by the Aussies, such as "no worries" and "shout" (for buying someone a drink), so she could tell her friends on our return.

We delighted in the many similarities and charming differences found in Australia. My brother's friends there were quite hospitable and we considered moving to Australia. Brenda's determined effort to find medical help surfaced in Sydney, where she sought in vain a consultation with an Australian internist recommended to her.

The joy of the trip was shattered immediately upon our return home. Our house had been damaged by the house sitter. He had allowed many people to stay there during our trip, against our instructions. Various items were stolen or broken, furniture was disfigured, and my car was damaged.

Our friends, family and neighbors didn't want to ruin our trip, so we were not alerted to what had happened while we were abroad. Brenda felt guilty and was enraged, since it had been her idea to have someone stay in the house, not wanting to impose on our neighbors to watch the house while we were gone. Her sanctuary had been violated.

Brenda's mother was staying with us following knee surgery when Nick and Sherrie treated us to a welcome home dinner a week after our return. Again Brenda drank too much, and she once more wrote a note saying she was tired of life and tried to take an overdose of pills at home that night.

By now I was used to looking for and listening to the signs of her suicide attempts and grabbed her early. After holding her on my bed for nearly two hours while her mother slept downstairs, she gradually calmed down and returned to her room to sleep. Once more she became herself when the alcohol and drugs in her system had diminished.

I insisted that we begin seeing the counselor again. I was trying to sell the real estate, but was afraid to leave her alone. She didn't feel the counselor was helping and instead went back to her family doctor and to a new chiropractor, an osteopath and another doctor in search of relief from her constant pain. Her family doctor gave her some audio cassette tapes about electroshock therapy, which he thought might help. She listened to them over and over and made extensive notes.

She travelled to visit Glenda in Fairfax, Virginia in May. I told Glenda and Fred about the two recent suicide attempts so they would watch her closely. I was glad she was gone and hoped she would stay awhile. I had grown weary of being her caretaker and needed time to organize a sales training company of my own and continue my attempts to sell our land hold-ings. I also needed some time to myself to think about our future together, thinking perhaps she and I might be better off going our separate ways.

When confronted by her sister about the recent suicide attempts, Brenda was mortified. She always wanted everyone to think well of her and would go to great lengths to cover up her condition. Glenda suggested she see a new psychiatrist when she returned.

My support was lukewarm, as I didn't think the doctors were helping her and I was tired of paying the bills. I was fed up with her constant ailments, chronic depression, and drinking problems.

While she was away, I attended an Al-Anon meeting on a hunch. Perhaps I would find answers on how to cure her. Instead, they talked about my need to cure me! I resisted that notion at first, but after a few meetings I realized I couldn't cure her and was only contributing to the problem with my own behavior. I began detaching myself from her behavior and working on my own new ways of coping with her and the world.

When she returned to Atlanta, we talked about divorcing to give us a new lease on life. We did agree to wait 90 days before deciding to do so to see if the doctors could come up with something. She had also agreed to attend an AA meeting whenever I went to Al-Anon, which I saw as a hopeful sign. However, she was obviously growing very desperate for help, grabbing at any straw.

I spent much of June trying to sell the land and attending Al-Anon meetings. Brenda went to several AA meetings but never believed she had a real alcohol problem. She continued her research on electroshock therapy, becoming convinced that shock treatment was the answer. She made an appointment in mid-July to see a new psychiatrist who was an authority on such therapy.

We spent July 4th with Nick, Sherrie and their children setting off fireworks and driving nearby to watch an extravagant music and fireworks display. Brenda wasn't happy with our vantage point and, after much complaining, forced us to move. I remarked to Nick that her temper tantrum was typical of what I had been going through with her. Ordinarily, she wouldn't have displayed such anger in front of her longtime friends. I didn't know it then, but the pressure inside her was building to the breaking point.

On July 8th, she attended her uncle's funeral. Strangely, she didn't want me to go with her. She wore a black blouse and checked slacks. She made comments to her relatives that day regarding what she wanted done if she were to die. I believe she didn't want me there because, had I heard her comments, I would have become alarmed that she was suicidal again.

The rest of that week she was up (manic). Brenda's mood swings occurred very quickly. Most of the time she was depressed, but during the manic phase she could accomplish a great deal. It frightened her when she was in a manic phase, because she knew she would soon plunge again into a depressed state.

Those last few days were filled with activities resembling real happiness for her. For the entire week, she displayed a feeling of determination to conquer her disease, thus easing the worries of those who loved her. She made a special effort to spend time with us and assure us that she was going to be all right. She was celebrating the last days of her life.

On Monday before her death, she spent some time with Sherrie, and they relived the goofy times of their youth during a day-long shopping excursion, giggling and joking as if they were 15 again. She rode the rapid transit that week, a first for her.

At the end of this happy day, Brenda reassured her longtime friend, saying "Sherrie, don't worry about me, I'm determined to conquer this thing. One day I'm going to know what it's like to wake up in the morning and not be afraid -- not worry about whether I'm going to be up or down. I'm going to find a way to control it. The diets and drugs haven't worked. After all the research on shock therapy I've done, I really think this is it. I'm not going to hurt myself. Don't ever worry about that again." That was the last time Sherrie saw Brenda.

That Tuesday, Brenda and I hauled Glenda and Fred's boat, which we had been storing in our garage, to a nearby lake where she drove it for the first and only time. She was kind to a stray dog at a Mexican restaurant that night, though she generally didn't like animals. Afterwards, we made love for the last time, though she was very tired.

Wednesday, July 11, we went to a friend's 40th birthday party. Brenda gave her black balloons as a present. The last picture of Brenda alive was taken that night. The picture shows how very tired she was. The next night was the Trivial Pursuit game at Dick and Gini's, and then came Friday the 13th and a full moon.

She dressed again in the black blouse and black checked slacks, which apparently she had chosen to die in, if the new psychiatrist couldn't help her. He refused the shock therapy and Brenda must have felt there was no other choice but suicide. She couldn't control her life, it seemed no one else could help, and so she controlled all that was left to her, her death.

Chapter 4

My First Months Alone

July - October, 1984

I believed Brenda might succeed in killing herself, so I presumed I was prepared for such a possibility. But my intellect does not control my emotions, even though I deluded myself to the contrary. The reality of her death proved that I had few skills to handle the emotional turbulence which permeated my whole being or to deal with the enormous void that had opened in my life.

Shock may not technically be called an emotion, but that's what I felt, or rather didn't feel, due to its numbing hold on me. Some part of me pulled the blanket of shock across my body to blot out my intense pain. Had I not been protected at first by shock, that agonizing ache might have driven me crazy.

Often during those first days without her, the pain infection inside me would boil through my numbness, giving some indication of battles I would fight with it in future days. When pain did creep out from under shock's covering, that protective blanket would quickly cover it up again. Shock is a survival mechanism, triggered by massive physical or psychological injuries, and not subject to our will. Otherwise, I wouldn't have been able to function, as I knew I must.

Much needed to be done. People were converging on "my" house the day after she died. Phone calls had to be made, particularly to Jay. Arrangements had to be discussed. Though sleepless, somehow I had to muster strength, and the numbness helped conserve what energy I had by covering up the pain.

Because of her preoccupation with death, Brenda had given me precise final instructions several times. She wanted her organs donated, though only her corneas were useable. She adamantly insisted on cremation, which was not her family's tradition. However, they didn't object when I made that wish clear. She also wanted us to remember the happy times, but that request would have to wait quite a while.

Few memories remain of her memorial service, except my almost constant crying, though I do remember being amazed at the number of friends and family who came that day. Crying wasn't allowed for men, the way I saw it, but those self-imposed restrictions were overwhelmed as I frequently lost control during the service. The woman who had been the center of my life was gone, and it hurt too much to not cry.

Julia told me she had typed a book by Iris Bolton about recovery from her own son's suicide. She said Iris led a Survivors of Suicide (SOS) support group at

48

The Link Counseling Center. I also have a memory fragment of my former secretary turning ghostly pale when she saw Brenda's twin sister at the funeral home.

Since we had to wait for the cremation process, the gravesite service was held two days later. As Brenda wished, the man who married us conducted both services, though he was visibly shaken. He had known the twins all his life, and had conducted marriage services for them. That day again was blurred through my tears.

I have very few conscious memories of the week after she died. Perhaps as the years go by I will remember more from those first crushing days without her, but for now that time is hidden somewhere in my mind. I do remember meeting a woman I've chosen to name Lisa while at a meeting with Penn to sell some of our land. She and her husband, whom I'll call Bob, would become very close friends.

Penn had invited me to come stay on their boat for a week or so. I wanted to take that time near the water, away from the house and all its memories, to begin dealing with the pain. I started crying as I left my driveway a few days after the service, and hardly stopped weeping the entire four-hour drive to Savannah. Long trips alone in cars, I learned later, are not recommended for early grievers, as our attention tends to wander from the road. After what seemed an eternity, I made it there safely.

I had bought Elisabeth Kubler-Ross's book, Questions and Answers on Death and Dying to read on the boat, along with the last two books Brenda read, Shirley MacLaine's Out on a Limb and Ruth Montgomery's A World Beyond. By then I was consumed with questions and hoped to find some answers in these books.

Why hadn't I seen the signs? Why didn't I care enough that week to project myself into her world of pain and darkness? Why had she left so finally and completely? Why had the new doctor failed to recognize her desperation? The books didn't answer these questions directly but offered many new ideas for me.

Penn introduced me to several books 14 years earlier about Eastern teachings, but I hadn't thought of their concepts of spirituality and reincarnation since then. At the time I put the possibility of past lives on my mind's shelf, not really pursuing the subject any further.

I found surprising consistencies between the MacLaine, Montgomery and Kubler-Ross books and those I had read years earlier. The ideas of many lives plus the certainty stated in all of them that life doesn't die with the body, provided me with hope.

And so I began my healing odyssey into metaphysics, which is the study of principles that transcend science. My search to learn more about myself and the unseen universe around me had begun. Little did I know then how very intertwined myself, metaphysics, and God really are!

Words and phrases either occurred to me or stayed with me from the books, as I wrote for me the following on the boat 11 days after Brenda's death:

"There is a power greater than me. I will use that power to adjust flaws in myself. The most immediate goal is to strengthen my self-image and feelings of self-worth. Next I must strengthen my natural empathy without buying other's problems. From these, I will become a more giving, caring person without feeling required to. I will accept help freely given, for I cannot do these things alone."

I would have many opportunities over the next five years to learn and relearn those lessons I wrote about. Some I am still learning.

As it always does, being near the water helped calm me. When it came time to leave, I was stronger and somewhat motivated to begin to learn and grow. Though I was depressed, I never really felt suicidal myself. What else could I do but go on?

I was in shock for many months. Thanks to Julia's suggestion, I did attend my first SOS meeting with Iris the month after Brenda's death. I believed those in the group could identify more closely with my feelings since those at Al-Anon still had their alcoholic alive.

The caring and compassion shown me that night from those strangers was an affirmation of the goodness we are all capable of giving. They understood what I was going through and did not mind my tears and inability to talk. I found I wasn't the only one who thought he had failed, and I learned that perhaps I hadn't failed at all.

As with Al-Anon support groups, I found this SOS group non-judgmental and truly supportive of my own emotions. The group has no real structure, unlike Al-Anon which is a 12-step program similar to AA. At SOS, we're not trying to learn a program. It is, rather, a warm supportive outlet where we can vent the overwhelming emotions that dominate our lives after suicide.

Iris gave us a handout that showed us suicidal indications in a loved one, for they give us many clues. Though knowing the signals after the fact temporarily increased my feelings of guilt, I was heartened that others might benefit if they knew the signs.

According to Iris, we should be alerted if one of our loved ones:

A. Talks about or threatens suicide. Such
   threats are a definite call for help, even if
   used to manipulate our behavior. A suicide
   attempt should always be taken seriously.

B. Repeatedly states he or she wishes they were dead or talks about death a lot.

C. Suddenly loses interest in favorite people, things, or activities.

D. Gives away prized possessions.

E. Suddenly changes behavior, including apparently getting much better.

F. Becomes extremely depressed (cries, can't sleep, loses appetite, seems hapless, hopeless, helpless).

G. Grows more isolated and despairing.

According to Iris, suicidal individuals are often either very dependent or very independent, perfectionistic, overly sensitive, angry (though often unable to express it), frustrated with themselves, and need to be liked. They may be extremely intolerant of injustice, unable to share feelings, manipulative towards others, seductive to others, highly impulsive, and very happy one minute and extremely depressed the next (manic-depressive).

Though Iris stressed that we cannot always prevent suicide, even when we know the signs, Brenda had displayed so many of these tendencies. So, I was assailed again by the "if only" and "what if" thoughts so common after someone chooses to die. For instance, "if only" she or I had known about Iris' work, or "what if" we had been aware that her suicide attempts were real attempts, not just a ploy for attention as I had been led to believe.

Perhaps by knowing what can happen to suicidal people we can try to convince them to get help. I believe that, through their knowledge and compassion, the people at The Link and other centers have convinced many suicidal people to go on living, to keep hope in their lives. Those of us who have had our lives altered by another's deliberate death cannot regain our lost loved one, but we might help convince someone else to choose life.

The support from SOS helped me face what would have been our 10th wedding anniversary August 17th. The group had said that anticipation of important days was often worse than the day itself. I wept a lot anyway on the anniversary that would be no more as I wallowed in the self pity that often broke through my shock.

"Ten years wasted," I thought. "Here I was, 43-years-old, starting over again. Why me? Why couldn't Brenda, my S.W., have been more considerate of what I would have to go through?" Fortunately, I remembered the valuable Al-Anon advice and made it through that day by taking a few minutes at a time.

September brought a new computer job, which included finding an office and hiring a staff. Negotiations were continuing on the sale of one of my land tracts. I also decided to treat myself to a new bed, thinking it was my bed that was causing my sleeplessness. It would take three beds and much struggle with the department store before I found the right one, since it really wasn't the beds that were causing my insomnia. It was my grief.

One night in late September after a church dinner I danced with a woman I will call Rachel. I felt instantly that I had known her before. She danced beautifully and we dated for awhile, but neither of us was ready for a relationship, particularly me. Compulsively, I wanted to be able to date again, but my grief emotions mixed with new love emotions were too confusing then.

Near the end of the month I finally negotiated a contract on one of the properties I had been trying so hard to sell. The buyer invited me over for dinner with his wife, his secretary Lisa, and her husband Bob.

Somehow the conversation that night drifted from Ayn Rand to metaphysics. Bob had lost his best friend to cancer just before Brenda died, so we were both grieving. We felt very comfortable talking together, even discovering we had the same birthday.

What a remarkable pair! Bob's great practical wisdom had been gained from many tribulations in his life. His sparkling, mischievous eyes, paired with a contagious warmth, complement Lisa's blond, bubbly cheerleader personality. "If there are soulmates," I thought, "these two new friends of mine certainly are qualified."

In October, I prepared to carry out one of Brenda's last requests and at the same time treat myself to a party. In the past (how hard it still was to think of her as gone) we often hosted an annual Halloween party. I decided to make our past tradition the occasion of drinking the toast to her she had requested in her last note. Brenda always felt that there should be joy in having known a departed loved one, and had said often that she wanted a party given in her memory if she should die.

I invited about 25 friends who felt strong enough to do so, to come and be part of this last ritual. I was apprehensive about my own strength and ability to carry out her request, feeling that others might not understand this "celebration." I imagined people saying "How dare he give a party this soon after his wife died!"

Unfortunately, Brenda's mother Grace was admitted to the hospital the Saturday before the party with a mild heart attack, adding worry over her health to my apprehensions about the party. I had grown close to Grace over the years, for she loved me unconditionally, treating me like a son. She, Brenda and I had travelled together often. I thought of her as part of my family. We had grieved together several times after our shared tragedy. She seemed to be recovering at the hospital, so I nervously went ahead with the party.

I assembled a collage of pictures of Brenda in costume, because she loved such parties, which I mounted on a wall before the guests arrived. My fears were unfounded about attendance, as nearly everyone showed up for the champagne toast to her memory she had requested. I tearfully said a few words about her before we drank to her life, which then was followed by a powerfully charged moment of silence.

Later that night, Brenda's brother called to say in a broken voice that his mother had suffered another very severe heart attack and wasn't expected to live. I was devastated. I had a house full of guests I felt responsible to and couldn't leave right away. Brenda's friend Sherrie, who had left the party for the hospital, called to tell me Grace had died. I asked the guests who remained to please leave.

Grace's death, coming just three months and two weeks after Brenda's, thrust me back unwillingly into the shock phase of grief. I also had profound guilt feelings about hosting the party the night her mother died. I wasn't prepared for this second great loss.

My background had not taught me about the now well-documented phases of grief over loss. The works of Elisabeth Kubler-Ross and Iris Bolton's book, My Son... My Son... have helped me to understand these phases. With knowledge of the grief process, it became easier for me to work through whatever phase gripped me at the time, and to better cope with losses since then.

The first phase of grief I experienced began with *shock*. My body and mind automatically shifted into this protective state that lasted quite a while, until I could begin to cope with the pain.

Along with the shock often came a *denial* that the loss had occurred. I pretended that nothing at all had happened, as I had the day after Brenda died and often thereafter.

I'm not sure I can describe to those of you, who haven't lived through a loved one's suicide, how intense and life-encompassing the pain is and how you want to pretend it didn't happen. In the process of denying the loss itself, I often denied the feelings that swept through me. I even may have denied Brenda's importance to me by trying to fill the emptiness by dating again a few months after her death, much too early (in hindsight).

There were many days when I would wake up and think her death was just a bad dream. Was my nightmare finally over? Then I would walk into her bedroom expecting to find her sleeping. When she wasn't there, the pain would surge back until the protective shock masked it again.

Denial was woven in with the shock during those early days because the loss was just too much to deal with then. It was easier to deny that my life had been shattered than to begin dealing with the pain of her death.

The combination of *shock* and *denial* precedes the next grief phase, *anger* and *depression*, mixed with other debilitating emotions. Many people never make it past this anger/depression phase. I believe some people refuse to acknowledge that anger is a normal reaction to loss. I even felt guilty sometimes about saying that I was angry about my loss.

The combination of angry feelings and deep depression make it very difficult to function at all, let alone think clearly. I often thought it wasn't appropriate to be selfishly angry that my love had left my life. I was just beginning to express my own anger over Brenda's suicide when her mother died.

I learned that guilt amplifies the anger and depression. Entire books have been written about this very destructive emotion. In suicide, guilt is intensified because of the deliberate nature of the death. I spent countless hours with "if only" and "should have," often berating myself for not anticipating this calamitous event.

In my case, I felt guilty about not saving Brenda, being alive myself, the mean things I had said to her, and the relief I sometimes felt because I wouldn't have to deal with her condition any longer. I don't think Grace ever acknowledged her anger or turned her guilt into healthier regret, which would have allowed her to glimpse the third and final phase of grieving, *understanding* (sometimes called *resignation*) and *acceptance.*

It is in this third phase of grief that I finally acknowledged the loss and began to live again. I came to terms with her death and accepted the reality of what had happened. However, this phase was not constantly with me until several years after she died.

I don't feel that anyone can avoid for long working through these steps, though some believe they never have to deal with anger to be able to understand and accept their loss. Many also bargain throughout the early grieving process, promising God or anyone else that they will do anything if their loved one is returned to them.

Suicide seems to bring out every negative emotion, sometimes with disabling intensity. In addition to the guilt, anger and depression, I was fearful of my now uncertain future. I was afraid of failing once more, afraid of being hurt again, and afraid of growing old alone.

I felt betrayed by the women close to me, since they had left me to fend for myself. I thought "How dare both Brenda and Grace leave me all alone!" It would be some time before I recognized and dealt with my paralyzing fear of abandonment.

Loneliness creeps into the grief cycle all the time, an ache especially acute when it is your spouse who has died. The empty nights and weekends became almost intolerable. Even in crowds, the feelings of abandonment and aloneness stole into my being.

It's also pretty common to feel bewildered, anxious, confused, doubtful and forgetful. My mind would just wander off at inopportune times, and I would forget even normal routine matters like paying bills and buying food. I would start out to do something and forget what it was I intended to accomplish. I would have thought I was going crazy, except the SOS group assured me I wasn't.

My whole body was plagued with an almost unbearable tension on top of my empty, sick heart. The stress usually settled into my back, which would ache almost constantly for years after she died. A great many of the remedies I sought, such as visiting chiropractors and meditating, centered around relieving my debilitating tension.

Occasionally, I was even ashamed that I had a wife who had killed herself, fearing this stigma would follow me for the rest of my life. When trying to date again the first two years after she died, I often felt this shame as I explained to new female friends that I had a suicidal wife who had finally succeeded. I was ashamed to have failed, and ashamed to have been in love with someone who couldn't face life.

An emotion often left out of grief literature is the forbidden one, hate. I found this feeling was one of the hardest to acknowledge because of the taboos surrounding it. There were times when I hated what Brenda had done, hated myself for failing, and hated other women when they left me, but it took me over four years to admit this emotion and express it, often by yelling around the house.

Another emotion not usually covered in the books about grieving, which I experienced often, was self-pity. As with most of the debilitating emotions, self-pity crops up throughout the grieving process. I frequently felt that I couldn't be loveable, that I was some sort of freak. I believed often that I had been unfairly treated by life.

I felt desperately sorry for myself and all the pain I was in. I was the victim of fate, cruelly cast out into the world again. I think even part of my martyrhood ("I can make it. Just look how strong I am!") was based in self-pity.

If feeling sorry for yourself goes unchecked, it can last for years. I was fortunate enough to have friends, counselors, and the SOS and Al-Anon support groups to gently keep me focussed on my goal to learn and grow, which made my bouts of self-pity short-lived. Most of the SOS group had been left no suicide note at all to comfort them, whereas I had a long, detailed, loving note, making my self-pity difficult to maintain.

Another emotion I still feel frequently is hurt. My wife left me, I felt I couldn't turn to my mother yet for support, and then Grace left me by dying. It does hurt when others let us down, and my wife's death is the biggest letdown I've ever experienced.

The teacher Lazaris says hurt is the only emotion that takes time to heal. He suggests that pain is a residual of hurt, and that any time we experience emotional pain we probably have unhealed hurt within us. I have found what he says to be true. Some of the hurt remains with me to this day, reinforced by losses I continue to experience as I try to find another mate.

Unfortunately, the grief process is not a straight line, though I wished it to be so. I moved in and out of the various phases in unpredictable ways.

For example, I often travelled all the way back to shock and denial when I saw someone at a shopping mall who resembled Brenda. Or, I returned to depression when I discovered something in a drawer that brought back memories of good times shared with her that would never be again. As time - the great healer - goes on, these slipbacks happened less frequently and with less severity, but it did help me to be ready for them by knowing they might occur.

Whatever emotions I dealt with were all amplified greatly by my pervasive state of grief. Even when positive emotions such as laughter or serenity poked through the dark wall of my grief, those emotions, too, were more intense.

Perhaps because of that intensity, I chose to suppress some of my grief by not crying, not stating my fears and regrets, not screaming my rage, and not expressing the other emotions normal to grief. Later I paid for this when those emotions came out, sometimes ferociously and too often directed at innocent bystanders, when another loss occurred in my life.

I believe suppressed grief emotions, which are profoundly intense, eventually affect our physical and mental health. Scientific studies seem to bear this out. Some very violent behavior has been shown to be encouraged by suppressed anger. Anxiety (often caused by unexpressed fear) apparently increases the chance of heart attack. Ulcers have been directly related to excessive worry.

Grace may have died of a broken heart, becoming trapped in the guilt, anger and depression phases of grieving. She couldn't express anger towards her daughter for killing herself. I became determined not to be trapped there myself, though denial of my feelings would continue to plague me for years.

Unfortunately, the night Grace died I began denying my own grief in an attempt to regain control of my life. I wanted to conquer the pain, and began to suppress my own feelings of loss. I was determined to move through the grief process, not allowing myself to express emotions that needed venting.

Nothing in my background, none of my training, none of my successes and failures had prepared me to deal with these overwhelming grief emotions. As with most people, my experience had taught me to deny and ignore my feelings. My journey through and beyond grief would change my experience as I learned to deal with emotions.

Chapter 5

Survival Continues

November & December, 1984

In the course of doing some promotional work for a remedial math teaching program a few years earlier, Brenda had met a woman I'll call Patty. They became friends immediately, seeming to have telepathy with each other.

When she and her husband, whom I'll call Howard, finally came to our house for dinner a few years before Brenda died, I was pleasantly surprised to find I had known him years earlier when I was married to Julia. He had been a member of my fraternity, when I was their advisor at Georgia State University. We had lost touch over the years. It seemed remarkably easy for the four of us to become good friends.

Patty combines traditional Midwestern warmth with a delightful enthusiasm that makes her a joy to be around. That is, unless she is crossed, in which case I'm glad we're long-time friends. Howard balances her attitude with a straightforward, facts-oriented approach to life, combined with a strong sense of justice. The four of us found we enjoyed each others' company.

They were particularly devastated by Brenda's death, since they had no inkling of her problems. We now shared our loss along with a mutual interest in metaphysics. They had attended a hypnosis workshop at Kennesaw College and suggested that I might find some help for my sleeping problem through hypnotherapy.

Though I felt I couldn't be hypnotized, I decided to give it a try. At my first meeting, I told the hypnotherapist I had two objectives - one, to be able to sleep normally and, two, to be able to get in touch with my intuition. She could tell I was stressed out, depressed and weary to the bone. She said she could help and conducted a relaxation hypnosis session immediately.

I felt that I had not really been hypnotized. I was fully aware of everything, and believed I hadn't lost control in any way. She patiently explained to me that most subjects react that way, and only a rare few actually go under so deeply that they lose awareness or control. She gave me a self-hypnosis tape and suggested I play it before trying to sleep. I did, and sound sleep began to follow. The soothing words and soft music on the tape were the drugless remedy I had been seeking.

I walked into my second session to find my hypnotherapist smiling and dangling her necklace in front of her. When I asked what she was doing, she said she was communicating with her inner self. "You want to get in touch with your intuition, don't you?" she said. The necklace, used as a pendulum, helped her intuitively to reveal we had known each other in several past lives.

I was intrigued. Here was another reference to past lives, this time involving a technique I could use to learn more specific information. I could perform my own research. If the pendulum worked for me, I could use it to communicate with my "intuition." She said I would be able to ask myself any question about this life or past lives.

She handed me her necklace, and, after a few instructions from her, the necklace began swinging for me! Was this really happening? I was amazed, because I wasn't consciously able to move it the same way by moving my hand.

The pendulum technique is very simple. Take any light weight at the end of a six-inch or so chain or string (my first pendulums were a small nail on a string and a safety pin on a thread) and hold the string or chain in the hand you write with a few inches from your heart. It helps to rest your elbow on a table or desk to keep the pendulum still. To protect yourself from any unwanted influences you may want to see yourself bathed in white light or pray for the highest guidance. Now ask any question about the past that

67

can be answered "yes" or "no" by the swinging of the pendulum.

Try something simple at first, such as "Is the sun shining outside?" If the pendulum swings towards and away from the body, the answer is "yes" in my case. If it swings side to side (left and right), the answer is "no." By practicing alone the swings may become more pronounced. Some people find for themselves that a different mix of swings means "yes" or "no," etc. Experimenting with it is the best way to learn for yourself.

I found out later that this ancient technique is one method of dowsing. People who find water under the ground for drilling wells also dowse, sometimes using a pendulum or a forked stick. If the pendulum works for you after some practice, you can use it to find lost objects, underground pipes and cables, perhaps even valuable ore veins or treasure, though I've never tried finding these myself.

I don't know how it works or why, but repeated testing showed the pendulum to be incredibly accurate for provable information. I now had a tool to use in my spare time to investigate past life data about people I knew, even though I still remained somewhat skeptical about the pendulum and the existence of past lives.

I was more excited than I had been at any time since Brenda's death! I could experiment with this tool, even with my doubts, to see if my conscious decisions agreed with my wiser inner self. Here was a way I could discover more about myself and the people in my life, particularly the new ones who continued to show up.

It would be a diversion from the many nights when I would just sit and stare. Oh, the television might be on, but all I could do was stare and suffer. This sitting and staring would come back to me many times over the years. It seems to be part of the depression that deep grief brings.

The hypnosis session that followed my pendulum lesson was almost anticlimactic, though my hypnotherapist proved I was hypnotized by telling me I wouldn't be able to get out of the chair until she brought me out of my light trance. She was right, the more I tried, the deeper I sank into the chair. I laughed for one of the few times since that black day in July.

However, I was still reeling from the blow of Grace's death, still anxious about Brenda's status, and concerned about my performance on the computer sales job. I visited a psychic in my search for relief from my anxieties. She assured me that Brenda continued to be cared for, her mother's spirit was doing fine, and that I was doing better than expected on the job.

I also asked her about several women I had met, but she said they would be just good friends. She saw new women coming into my life, but had no details. She also verified that the pendulum was a very good way to get in touch with my inner self and explore past relationships.

I was reassured and much more at peace after the session. Her caring advice gave me some much needed peace of mind, though I held on to some skepticism about psychic phenomena.

On my first Thanksgiving without Brenda, I travelled to visit Glenda, Fred and their children. We were all still in shock over our two recent losses, and we did what we could to comfort each other. Their company brought me solace and a feeling of belonging, and gave me some hope that at least part of Brenda's family would survive. They were determined to go on with their lives in spite of their pain, and were a real inspiration to me.

I remember showing their children the pendulum as an amusing pastime. As small, bright children will do, the youngest daughter's second question of the pendulum was "Is there a God?" The answer, of course, was "yes." Children seem to have a way of asking the most important questions, a trait I decided to get back in touch with as part of my learning and growing.

The next weekend back in Atlanta I met a friend of Bob and Lisa's I will call Marie. I felt immediately that I had known her before. The pendulum told me she was a karmic soulmate, which may explain why I did not initially feel comfortable with her, since karmic implies unresolved actions and emotions from previous lives together.

I decided to discover how many soulmates I could identify with the pendulum. My impression had been that we have one true soulmate, though the Jess Stearn book Soulmates implied there could be more than one. The pendulum indicated I had met no less than 10 soulmates in my life, and I had met five since Brenda died!

The first two were my college sweethearts, with whom I had lost touch. The third soulmate was the Southern belle I had dated in Atlanta in late 1963, who was now divorced and a friend again. Next came my first wife Julia (a twin soulmate and therefore one with close ties from the past), then Brenda, who was a twin and karmic soulmate, then Rachel, Marie and three new acquaintances.

On my next visit to the psychic, I asked if she could shed some light on my quandary of having known 10 soulmates. There was no way I could try to date the seven I was in contact with, since I was having a hard enough time just trying to learn how to date again. She said these soulmates were only here to help me through my grief, an intervention to fill a gap. She saw no long term relationships with them other than friendship, and said they would be phasing out of my life in about six months. I would come to wish I had paid more attention to her prophecy several months later, for I would have been better prepared for losses to come.

My metaphysical book reading continued that December, with the most influential works being Dr. Raymond Moody, Jr.'s <u>Life after Life</u>, Jane Roberts' <u>Seth Speaks</u>, and <u>Messages From Michael</u> by Chelsea Quinn Yarbro. I would have read more books on grief recovery then, but there were very few. Those I had read rarely dealt with recovery from suicide. Besides, my fascination with psychic phenomena engrossed me to the point of forgetting that I had grief work yet to finish.

I was particularly interested in the similarity between clinical research done on near-death experiences and the messages supposedly coming from "beings" after death. Hypnotized subjects recalling supposed death experiences from a previous life, patients clinically dead who had been revived, and entities speaking from the other side through mediums all told of very similar experiences.

They described spiritually rising above the body, hearing a noise such as a buzz, travelling through a dark tunnel and meeting a "being" of light. In my state of grief, I was immensely comforted by this evidence of life after death. Not only did I now feel my father, Brenda, and her mother Grace were still living in another dimension, I also felt certain my spirit would go on when I died. I <u>would</u> see my loved ones again. I was coming to the conclusion, reached by so many over the ages, that life is eternal, though the body inevitably dies.

But I still wondered "Where was that eternal life spent? Was it in heaven or hell?" All my life I had never been comfortable with traditional concepts of heaven and hell. Having only two choices when we die always seemed too cut and dried for me. There must be a grey area, somewhere in between.

I was becoming more and more convinced from my studies that what we see after we die is what we want to see, or believe we will see, and not the gates of heaven or hell we're so often told about. In fact, according to these writings, there are many levels of existence we go to after death. Any decision regarding our own appropriate level would be made by our higher, inner self, which many of the writings said is a part of God.

It was appropriate to have thoughts of God as the Christmas season approached. I was finally beginning to understand what a truly miraculous man Jesus was. His teachings would become more important to me as time went on. His example of unconditional love is often missed in our Christmas celebrations, not to mention everyday life.

Brenda had not enjoyed Christmas, believing the holiday time was an even bigger strain than the rest of the year. As many psychotherapists know, the holiday season is particularly rough on depressed people.

She and Jay were also allergic to Christmas trees, making the season physically uncomfortable for them. Our anger, depression and frustration during Christmases together had permeated the household while Jay lived with us. Before they came into my life, I had usually enjoyed Christmas and couldn't understand their problems with this time of year.

To try and put more joy in the holiday season after Jay moved to California, Brenda, her mother and I had traveled to Virginia to be with Fred, Glenda and their children during the 1982 and 1983 holidays. In 1984, Fred and Glenda decided on a cruise to change their scenery and distance themselves from the tragedies for awhile.

Therefore, I was on my own for the holidays with my thoughts and feelings, desperately missing Brenda and her mother. My brother and his wife were on their boat in the Caribbean, and I was re-establishing the relationship with my mother. Silently I wailed "How will I survive this Christmas without so many of the people who had shared the time with me just a year ago?"

Oh, the loneliness I felt! That desperate feeling of being by myself struck with a vengeance. Even when I was around people, I felt alone. Now most of my supportive friends and family were away during this very critical holiday season.

Since I had so many soulmates and so many new friends in my life, though, I needn't have worried. I stayed very busy. Plans seemed to materialize every night but two from the SOS meeting December 12th until New Year's Day.

Keeping busy left little time for the amplified depression typical for those of us in deep grief during the Christmas holidays. These are the times we took photographs of in the past, where giving and sharing together were traditional. Thus these are the times when we most miss those we've lost.

I was very anxious to have the new year roll in. I wanted to be able to say "My wife died last year." I felt I might be more normal if I could convince myself that my losses happened last year.

I'm sure those close to me found it hard to deal with me as I was then, appearing to be fine one minute and crying the next. It seems people feel more comfortable around us if enough time has passed after our tragedies. Then, they wouldn't be forced to deal with the roller coaster emotions we often exhibit.

Three functions on Christmas Day kept me busy enough so only a few tears flowed. My anxiety about making it through that day turned out to be worse than the day itself really was, as I had been told at SOS.

Bob, Lisa and Marie took me to dinner and a comedy show on Bob's and my mutual December 28th birthdays. I even laughed at the comedy sketches. I went to a New Year's Eve party with Marie and her friends. That helped some, since I didn't have to be around the friends Brenda and I had in common, who would have brought back memories.

Though I didn't feel much like saying "Happy New Year," I was glad 1984 was history. I had managed to cope for nearly six months and was more than ready to face the challenges of my job, establishing some sort of female relationship and further healing in 1985.

Chapter 6

New Year, New Losses

January - June, 1985

My counselor had advised me that there might be transitional relationships for me as I healed. These are romances that don't last, but are beneficial in the struggle to find a new identity after a long-term relationship ends. I was fortunate to have two of these early, the short one with Rachel and the developing one with Marie.

She gave me Richard Bach's <u>The Bridge Across Forever</u> for Christmas, a book about his quest for a soulmate and his stumbling blocks along the way. This one was very special to me for several reasons: because she knew how much I wanted it, though we didn't know each other very well yet; because I had loved his previous books; and because I had lost one soulmate and found another one in her.

I started really caring deeply for Marie the weekend of January 12th. I'm noted for being frugal, and on the previous Thursday had mixed a can of old oysters I found in my refrigerator with a can of oyster stew. While stirring the soup, it looked pretty grey and unappetizing, but my frugality won and I ate the soup anyway.

The next few days I was dashing to the bathroom more often than freeway stops occur during highway rush hour, thanks to the thoroughly tainted oysters. She didn't make fun of my self-imposed predicament. On top of this indisposition, I frequently developed what she called "leaky eyes" over the weekend and in the weeks ahead. It was still a time of crying for me and she understood. I loved her for that understanding, and for caring how I felt.

The rest of January was filled with computer work, quality time with her and extensive pendulum investigations. Since it only works with "yes" and "no" questions, gathering data on past lives is tedious. It was, however, a most rewarding hobby, for it gave me that precious commodity - hope. And, pendulum questioning is done best alone, which was my condition most weekday nights.

I was now beginning to appreciate my alone times, though they were sometimes very painful. I hadn't realized how hectic my life had been before with two jobs on top of Brenda's, Jay's and my own problems, and how much of my life was spent doing what others wanted me to do. I still missed my wife daily and missed having someone in the house. But, my time was my own, to manage as I saw fit. For the first time in my life I embraced my solitude instead of planning some activity to avoid being alone.

Living alone meant I could get up at 3 AM and eat ice cream while watching television without fear of disturbing anyone. Fortunately, I wasn't often awake at that time, thanks to the hypnotherapy tapes and the right bed, finally. That time of night is perhaps the loneliest of hours, particularly when you're depressed.

I asked Bob, Lisa and Marie over for dinner. It felt good to have warm, supportive people in the house again, a welcome break in my weeknight solitude. I began to feel more like a normal person and less like a freak.

Since February is usually a dull month, and I was feeling more positive, I decided to invite all of my friends who were interested in metaphysics to come to my house. Twenty came, and the feelings that night in the house were some of the warmest I could remember experiencing. Virtually everyone agreed they felt the same way.

The next weekend Bob, Lisa, Marie and I went to Gatlinburg, Tennessee for a long weekend of relaxed fun. The house we rented had a spectacular view of the mountains and the town below. The shared compatibility between the four of us served us well that weekend, as we frolicked in the snow and enjoyed the restaurants and shops. It felt wonderful to laugh and just have fun for a change.

Soon after, Marie met me in Miami for a rendezvous during a long business trip through Florida for me. The sun, sea and her company were exhilarating, but I had chosen to stay at a motel Brenda and I had enjoyed, thinking I could replace old memories with new ones. I had unconsciously been trying to do this on other occasions with her and hadn't considered her feelings.

I wasn't aware that much of my anger at Brenda's death was surfacing, or that I dealt with the anger by directing it subtly at other women. My passive aggressiveness was surfacing again. I thought I had cured myself of this tendency to be nasty while acting nice by working with my counselor.

She drew away from me during the weekend after I chose to sleep in a separate bed, partly because I was sunburned and restless. My reaction to her distant behavior was to feel rejected, which turned me into a silent sufferer (a passive-aggressive and codependent trait). Rather than confront the distance between us, we spent most of Sunday not speaking. The fun had evaporated.

After hours of the silent treatment and lonely walks on the beach away from each other, we tried to talk it out. Attempting to express my feelings in words was new and difficult for me, since I had normally suppressed so many feelings. I felt I was the injured party (sometimes called martyrhood), thus none of our ensuing discussions worked. She left my car at the airport still mad.

It wasn't until much later she told me what had happened that weekend reminded her too much of a past relationship in her life. She felt rejected when I slept in a separate bed. Both of us, it seems, were playing old behavior tapes, rather than dealing honestly with our feelings and each other in the moment.

I returned from the long Florida trip to find a potential buyer waiting for the last tract of land. I showed him the property the next day and prospects looked good for putting that duty-bound phase of my life behind me. I was beginning to realize that much of my life had been spent performing duties, a habit shared by many codependents. Duty is something one is morally or legally bound to do. My perception of life had been a trained response to a sense of duty, rather than doing what I felt like doing. As a result, I permitted very little joy in my life.

I allowed others to manipulate me, rather than choosing to take my own actions. I was disentangling myself from the duties associated with Brenda, her mother, my mother, and the land. I was beginning to learn that my first duty was to my own happiness and peace-of-mind. I was finally doing what I wanted to do.

In early March, my new rose bushes arrived. Here was pleasure, not a duty. How I enjoyed their beauty!

Our second year in the house, I had bought a two-dollar K-Mart rose bush and planted it between two pine trees. The neighbors said roses didn't do well in our neighborhood, and especially not under pines. To my surprise, the bush flourished with the most beautiful Double Delight blooms.

The Double Delight is one of the prettiest blooms in the world, with a white and yellow center, red petal tips and a heavy rose fragrance. That bush led to my planting 80 more, and now here were 20 new ones. I garden because I want to, not because I have to. I couldn't wait to get the new bushes in the ground!

Brenda loved the roses, as have many others. While watering the roses some months after her death, an astonishing event happened to me. While she was alive, I would often work in the yard as she slept late in the morning. When she did wake up, she would often come out to our back patio and call my name in a tentative, half asleep, questioning tone.

That day in March, I heard the same voice over my shoulder as I watered bushes with my back to the patio. For a few seconds, I didn't think much of it until I remembered she was dead. I had heard of such imaginings by survivors, but her voice sounded very real to me. Could it have been her?

After some thought, I realized perhaps she had come awake on the other side of death and was baffled. Her spirit may have returned briefly to her sanctuary. I turned, but she was not there, and again I sadly realized how much I would miss experiencing her delight in the spring blooms, particularly the roses.

The next night, I met with Rachel, whom I hadn't seen in awhile. She had loved the roses I always brought when we had dated. We had both come a long way in our healing separately, and I felt loved in her presence. We decided to try to date again.

April 23 was Brenda's birthday, with the anticipation of the day far worse than the day itself. I sent a card to Glenda, but that didn't really fill the empty day. As with all the other days since she died, this one finally passed.

Soon after, I hosted a second party for my metaphysical friends. Marie spent a long time talking to my psychological counselor that night, for she was interested in working with a group in some capacity and he was thinking of forming one. I knew he needed a female co-leader. I was busy being host and talking to my friends and didn't pay too much attention to their time spent together.

I went sailing blythely into May forgetting completely my history of problems during that month. I had also forgotten the psychic's prediction that my soulmates would be leaving my life in six months.

Julia and I had come to the end of our marriage in May of 1971. Brenda and I fought often during May. Before our marriage, we had almost parted for good in May. She would often take trips by herself that month, perhaps to get away from my foul moods at that time of year.

On May 1, I closed the sale of the first of the three tracts of land, with the second tract closing the next day. I was ecstatic and depressed at the same time. I was about to be rid of this albatross, but Brenda would not be with me to celebrate. The loneliness of my grief crept into my life again, in spite of my land sales successes.

I was working too hard at too many tasks, with the computer job, selling the land, dating two women, maintaining the house and grieving. Grief is very hard work in itself, the hardest work I have ever done.

I had been told about grief being work, but forgot that many other areas of my life were also work. I was overloaded and needed to simplify my life, so I decided to start by resigning from my computer job, which I did.

The day before, Julia had remarried, to someone she said she really loved. I felt happy for her. The night I resigned, I treated Marie and myself to dinner and the opera. I was in a great mood, for I saw a summer of freedom from the business of selling computers and land. I would be free to play with Marie and Rachel and to do what I wanted to do.

I had developed a love for opera over the years of escorting my mother and grandmother. I wanted to share the joy, one of the few I had allowed myself, with my new love, as I had previously with Brenda and Julia. There is a majesty and hypnotic reverie I experience listening to the live, highly-trained voices while watching the splendor of grand opera on stage.

During the intermission, I spotted some friends of Brenda's and mine. I believed they didn't know she had died, so I excused myself to tell them the sad news. They were shocked and gave their condolences.

When I rejoined Marie she seemed very distant, which I had come to know meant she was angry about something. Apparently she thought I was dwelling too much in the past by wanting to tell my story to old friends. Driving to her car later, I became furious after she called me by another man's name.

Thinking her attitude incredibly insensitive, I phoned her the next day to cancel our next date. Just who did she think she was, not wanting me to tell my friends of our mutual loss, then insulting me by calling me someone else's name?

I felt devastated. My longest relationship since Brenda's death hadn't worked out. Though we continued to date, I knew intuitively that the rekindled bond with Rachel would end soon, too. About that same time, I learned that two more of my other soulmates were dating younger men. Another lonely period loomed before me.

Self-pity overtook me again. I was now 44-years-old, considered myself over-the-hill and felt unable to attract women who would stay in my life. Where was the woman I needed to validate myself?

Why did women keep leaving me, abandoning me to my loneliness?

Finally, I remembered the psychic's prediction that my soulmates would be phasing out, and she had been absolutely right. What uncanny power of prediction she possessed! But her accuracy didn't make me feel any better. My hoped-for summer of fun and dating had been torpedoed.

Around that time, I wrote and posted on my refrigerator door the following sayings, reflective of my feelings of worthlessness:

"Expect nothing, and you will not be disappointed.

When in doubt, stop feeling and think.

Molehills cannot become mountains without my help.

Be sure you're right, then keep your mouth shut.

Don't take anything seriously, particularly yourself."

The breakup with Marie, quitting my job, and the anticipated loss of Rachel had thrown me once again into grieving over loss. Since I was still dealing with my deep earlier grief, these new losses were more intensely felt, again opening my barely-healed "soul" wound. My feelings of loneliness, fear, hurt, envy, self-pity and anxiety returned with a vengeance.

I wasn't feeling comfortable with, nor confident after, my sessions with my psychological counselor. So I tried a session with a psychic counselor named Jackie Woods, who had been recommended to me by friends. During the first visit with this remarkable healer, she confirmed that my problems were tied to some of the attitudes and feelings I had learned from and harbored toward my mother. She began a series of sessions to help me break free from my past.

At one of those sessions Jackie pinpointed my troubles with women in May to a previous life. Apparently a son I had loved dearly had died in May, and I felt his mother had neglected him. I still carried that resentment and would vent it each May towards the nearest female.

After this first visit, I had lunch with my mother, after which we visited my grandmother who was in a nursing home. Afterwards I was the target for an angry blast from my mother.

I realized for the first time my mother couldn't help herself unless she wanted to, and her desire to do so was not my responsibility. Besides, she was very upset at her own mother's failing health, so much of the anger wasn't really directed at me, but was normal frustration from seeing my grandmother declining.

The next Saturday began a long string of dateless or unsatisfyingly shortened-date Saturdays. Evidently this was to be a time for lonely introspection for me. Eventually, I began to accept my times alone as a chance to look inward.

My thoughts turned to the lost relationship with Marie, which clearly was a transitional one for both of us. From our talks I realized I wanted more commitment, she wanted more freedom. Jackie also pointed out to me a tendency I have to make other people's decisions for them and even sometimes finish their sentences for them, which I later found is a codependent way of behaving.

Another trait I became aware of from Jackie, also a codependent one, was jealous possessiveness, caused by my fear of being alone and my low self-esteem. Looking back on my life, that strangling jealous clutch ended or severely damaged many of my relationships.

The closing of the last piece of property in June finally freed me of the real estate burden. That same day I travelled alone to stay again on Penn and Kitty's boat for a long weekend. The water and change of scenery helped me regain some balance.

Upon my return home, I hosted a large party to celebrate the land sale. I invited new friends and old, but had no date myself. That party sadly reminded me again of how very much I missed my wife. She was a brilliant hostess, though parties always tired her out.

Brenda was not there to celebrate the end of the long cash drain, which had lasted through our entire relationship. Though she had been gone almost a year, that night her death seemed like yesterday again.

Marie came to the party as just a friend now, but left early without saying goodbye. Strangely, my psychological counselor left at the same time. At lunch together the next week, she asked numerous questions about the counselor. I finally got the message, later confirmed by friends. They were dating each other!

I was incensed, awash with a feeling of absolute betrayal. How could they do this to me? Why had they let me down so? I had decided earlier that Jackie was helping me cope, so I cancelled my last appointment with my psychological counselor.

The final loss came near the end of June. I had invited Rachel over for dinner, but she left early, angry at my discussing the recent betrayal. She had enjoyed my being romantic, taking particular delight in the roses I brought her and the messages I wrote on the cards I sent her, but she couldn't understand my need to date more than one person.

I didn't blame her for leaving, but my sadness deepened as I watched her leave my life. My summer plans were not turning out at all as I had hoped. All of my soulmates were gone, leaving me alone and grieving again.

My depression deepened, for I knew I had to face the anniversary of Brenda's death alone. I raged inwardly that neither Brenda nor Marie nor Rachel would share with me this summertime of freedom from duties. I still codependently looked to others for my happiness.

Chapter 7

The First Year Ends

July - December, 1985

Early in July I visited an astrologer named Sheila Conrad to investigate this area of metaphysics. I dreaded the approaching anniversary of Brenda's death, and I wanted to understand what the stars and planets had in store for me.

She found that my moon sign is the same as my sun sign, Capricorn, with my ascending sign in Leo. This all sounded fine to me, considering I knew nothing about astrology. She said I have two planets in Sagittarius and three in Taurus, which seemed to explain my affinity for Brenda, Marie and Rachel, to some extent, since Brenda's and Rachel's sun signs were Taurus and Marie's Sagittarius.

Sheila told me that from birth I had struggled with a great conflict. On the one hand I had a strong desire to be very individualistic, but on the other hand I wanted to be proper, traditional and conforming. I would tend to go back and forth between being a loner and joining groups. How right she was! All my life I have struggled with these conflicting desires.

Sometimes I really want to be with people, to work or play together for mutual satisfaction. At other times, I prefer being alone, with no one around to alter what I am doing, thinking, or feeling. Many people I know see me as a congenial group member, while others see me as a solitary person.

I have always fluctuated between wanting to be alone and enjoying group activities, so Sheila's planetary insight impressed me. She also saw me in a time of looking forward then, but would enter a time of looking backward in late November, words I was to remember later.

I do believe planetary influences affect behavior, particularly the full moon. My research revealed a marked increase in violent crime, births and suicides during a full moon. Brenda had tried to kill herself under the full moon of March, 1984, and had succeeded the following July.

On Friday, July 5, Bob, Lisa, Howard, and Patty gathered at my house for dinner. Afterwards, we talked about automatic writing, a technique used by Ruth Montgomery and others for communicating with spirits on the other side of life. Basically, using either a writing instrument or typewriter, the person writing automatically goes into a trance state and lets words flow through them onto paper.

Lisa thought perhaps someday she would like to try it. I said "Why not now?," and after much joking and persuasion, we placed my typewriter in front of her. We lit some candles and sat quietly meditating.

After 15 minutes, nothing had happened. Then, for some reason, I said, "Start typing" and she did. With her eyes closed, she typed:

Now is the time for you to get on with your life. I don't care about the house now. It doesn't mean that much anymore. I think I've gotten a little wiser now, don't you? Brenda

I was astonished! Lisa had never met Brenda nor seen her last note, but there was Brenda's phrase "Get on with your life." Brenda had been devastated by the damage done to our home by the house sitter, but Lisa wasn't aware of that. Also, she didn't know I had been praying constantly that my lost love would find peace and wisdom where she was.

A warm glow came over my entire body as I thought excitedly that here was real proof, to me, that Brenda lived. Something wonderful happened to me as I saw that short message just one week before the anniversary of Brenda's death.

Lisa then "typed" a message from Bob's best friend, who had died of cancer a few weeks before Brenda killed herself. Again, statements were typed that only Bob really knew about. Either Lisa was a reader of our minds, impressive in itself, or she was truly communicating with our loved ones! She was the most skeptical of all, though she was glad she had been able to help Bob and me.

We gathered again on the anniversary of Brenda's death, this time at Howard and Patty's house. We all were to spend the night so Bob and Lisa wouldn't have their long drive home and so I wouldn't be in my house alone overnight.

Though I was very sad that night, I shared my excitement over another book I was drawn to buy and read the week before. I told them that on page 17 of Brad & Francie Steiger's book The Star People they mentioned that the activating phrase for such people, whose origin may be from the stars, is "Now is the time," which were the first words of Brenda's message the week before.

Apparently, the phrase "Now is the time" is meant to get us started on our life's mission. Had I really started on mine? Had Brenda's death and the typed message from her meant that my real life's mission was beginning? If so, what on earth was that mission?

Lisa typed again for us that night. The message from Brenda was curt:

Nothing to say, Jack. There's no point. Get on with it. Brenda

Lisa also typed messages from two grandfathers and Bob's friend. Though tired, at around 2:45 AM, Lisa apparently contacted my deceased father, who sent a truly enlightening message:

Dear, dear Jack ....When will you learn to accept the fact that your mother will never be pleased with any of her men? Not totally. I don't justify her attitude and actions, which lately have not been up to my standards, if you will.

Don't let this seemingly bitter attitude make you feel responsible because it absolutely has nothing to do with you. Her kind of peace has to come from within. Realize this and the burden will become lighter. I know that the past year has taken its toll on you emotionally. If only she could search as you have in this past year for some kind of solitude.

Pray for her but stay away from such negative feelings, as they can only destroy what you have been building this past year. I love you, Jack, and do watch over you more than you may realize. Just remember this and while I am looking after you, would you please say a prayer for your dear old Dad? Thanks Son, I know your friend is tired but sometimes, let's get together for a longer session and ask me specific questions if you wish.

What a wonderful gift! The style was my father's, right down to the request for a prayer and calling me "Son," as he did when he was being serious with me. Even more precious, I had insight into my mother's state-of-mind that was to further change my entire attitude towards her. From that day on, I would treat her with more compassion and understanding. I hoped her peace would come from within as I began to accept her as she was.

He had requested that I "take care of your mother" before he died. I had always done so to the best of my ability, driven by my strong sense of duty, though I could never seem to do enough (codependents never can). His message gave me some relief from the obligation I felt, and began what would become a very strong, adult friendship with my mother.

I could now say my wife had died over a year ago. The night at Howard and Patty's brought back the tears and memories, but the first anniversary wasn't as traumatic as I expected. I now felt that life after death was a reality, and I strongly believed my lost love was learning on her "side of the veil" as I was on my side.

I just drifted most of the summer, attending occasional parties, going to various classes and reading extensively. My garden provided many hours of pleasant labor as the plants continued to flourish. I also enjoyed being free of the constant pressure of the corporate computer world.

One night in August at Bob and Lisa's home, the three of us discovered that his departed friend was one of his guides during another message typed by Lisa. We also received the following message from an entity named "Schuster." I'd been told by the psychic and my pendulum that he was one of my guardian angels (or guides):

I am Schuster. Let it be known that I do not wish anyone harm or wish to take over a body. It hasn't been my choice in the past and I do not wish to break the mold now. An old dog does not learn new tricks and so with me.

So much for my introduction. Jack, you are a joy to work with. I must say you keep us, and especially me, on our toes with all of your questions, but I am glad to have the opportunity to work with someone who has opened up to the spiritual world and is ready to accept new thoughts that may sometimes seem to be unspeakable or unheard of. You really haven't seen anything yet.

I know that in possessing the earth body that you have, you have for many years forgotten what it was like when you were in the spirit world, so you're trying to relearn what you already know. It's unfair sometimes, it seems, because you were so alert and ready, willing and able to accomplish your goals when you were here.

But the earth body makes it sometimes impossible for people to get back to the spirit world....and those religious groups that preach their dogma....what a shame. If you ever question your own growth, look at the people that never think outside of the Sunday church service.

I want you to know that I think you are a joy to work with. Try to be more intuitive. By this I mean, listen to your thoughts, your gut feelings and own common sense and our communication will become much easier. You will become as your friend Lisa and will be able to communicate with me.

Meditation is a good way to get within your-self and it comes down to basically clearing your mind of the garbage that seems to infiltrate the senses. Besides, the pendulum takes a lot longer. Why write a letter when you can just pick up the phone? It's not hard, and what harm can come? I only want to help.

Some of the guides here have people that don't listen to them and sometimes I feel bad because I have a sponge for a subject and I really appreciate the opportunity to be with you. Your friend is a good person and I will communicate through her if you find that it isn't very easy for you in the beginning. Good luck, good day.

If Lisa was making all this up she sure was giving me good advice. But I didn't see how she could be faking it, considering Schuster's style was quite different from other messages she had typed. Besides, she did not know that my pendulum had told me earlier that Schuster had never been incarnated on Earth. I really had a wise guardian angel guiding me, in addition to my father, who was also guiding me then.

Lisa called the next day to say she felt I should sell my house. I had put off such a decision until I was stronger, but now I really had to consider it. Was my home haunted by my dead wife's spirit? Were there too many reminders in the house of her for me to be happy there? Where would I move? Could I stand the strain of moving?

After much thought and deliberation, I decided to stay in the house for awhile, mainly because I didn't feel strong enough yet to go through the trauma of selling and moving. Besides, I had worked hard on the house and gardens and wanted to enjoy them. I planned to travel when and if the house was sold and wasn't ready yet to take off. I wanted to travel with someone I really cared for and that person wasn't in my life.

Late that summer I journeyed to Virginia to see Fred and Glenda and the children. On the way, I stopped to see a woman friend in Charlotte, North Carolina. She was a good dancer, so we went dancing that Saturday night, breaking my long jinx of no Saturday night dates.

I learned an important lesson with her. For the first time in my life, I didn't feel I had to be in control of time spent together. I wasn't upset when we did what she needed to do instead of what I wanted to do. I was learning to be more at ease with myself, thus I could be more at ease with others.

We discussed my extensive research into my past lives and the idea of this book began to form. Peeling the layers from this life and others had helped me heal, and maybe my experiences might help others recovering from loss. My work with the pendulum, hypnotic regressions and input from psychics had given me a fairly detailed picture of my past lives. My friend seemed fascinated.

Not wanting to scare her away, I suggested she think of my findings as a hobby that I used for my own healing - a fantasy if she chose to think so. If I wrote a book, its purpose would be to show that there is a full and rich life after losing someone you love but not to prove reincarnation.

My research revealed 40 past lives, with many people I know now. It seems I was a woman in only three of them, another indicator that there is work to be done by me in relating with females. I never really cared whether I was rich or famous in any of them. My guess is I was a very humble human being in most, if not all, of them.

Knowledge about past lives does help explain many current situations that don't seem to respond to psychological counseling. For instance, I came to a much better understanding of my mother using past life techniques. I discovered a pattern of long-standing associations between us with me as the subordinate (that is, as her son, for instance, and she as mother or father). It was clear to me that we needed to treat each other as equals from now on.

The theory of past lives also explained why so many new friends had been so helpful in my recovery. It seemed we had spent many lives being close in a variety of relationships (parent, child, friend, sibling, lover, etc.), enabling us to identify on more levels than most people I knew or met. For instance, Bob, Lisa, Howard and Patty and I had spent many lives together. The soulmates and new friends that came into my life so quickly, answering my silent screams for help, had also shared many of my lives.

My past life investigations had kept my mind occupied during some very lonely and sad months. But I had a life to live more fully now. I hoped my now firm belief in past lives would serve as an occasional reference point for me to live in the present.

Life is learning to love, and past lives only give us some glimpse of why we initially care or don't care for certain people. It is love that rescues us from being alone, love of ourselves and those around us, without conditions or expectations. Perhaps the conditions and expectations we impose on love diminish our ability to love.

My return from Charlotte began a three-month period when I found some happiness again. Many of my friends had been commenting about the changes in me. I was more relaxed, better able to have fun and more pleasant company for those around me. I was finally getting on with my life, living in the present more often than in the past or future.

Jackie, my psychic counselor, said I was truly opening up, but still needed to deal with some aspects of my loss. She also said we create our own reality with the way we see and react to our lives. Since I have a tendency to ignore advice, I promptly forgot what she said for the next three months. I think I was still resisting the concept that what we visualize, what we expect, is often what we get.

We began interpreting my dreams as a way of discovering what was going on in my higher conscious self. She warned of a fogging of my purpose in late November and again advised me to have some fun, go with the flow, and stop pushing so hard. She also saw a woman coming into my life, but said it wasn't time for this woman to reveal her feelings.

I hosted a Columbus Day party for my growing list of friends interested in metaphysics and for the first time had fun at my own party. I didn't run the party as I had in the past, I simply let everyone fend for themselves. I didn't feel a need to control the party.

I dated someone that autumn who was one of the only women who asked me over for dinner several times. I was surprised that this old custom had seemingly died out while I had been married. It would be awhile before I would realize that perhaps I had been dating women who weren't good for me.

The first week in November, I visited the side-by-side gravesites of Brenda and Grace. I don't go there often, for I know their spirits are elsewhere, but occasionally such a journey gave me comfort and another measure of release. Any lingering denial that they were dead was answered by the sober reality of the grave markers.

I also had some releasing of the past to take care of at the gravesite that day. Some months before, while cleaning what had been Brenda's room, I had discovered a skull fragment. I had carefully added that fragment to some hairs of hers I had found and placed in my drawer.

I had read that holding on to such particles of a loved one's body could delay my grief recovery and might hold her back, so I dropped the fragment and hairs at the gravesite that day. It was another symbolic gesture of letting go and moving on. I wasn't as emotional this visit, realizing on the way home that I was gradually releasing my past.

The next week, I travelled alone to hear the well-known teacher Ram Dass speak. Earlier in his life, he had worked with Dr. Timothy Leary on some experiments with mind-altering drugs, but had discovered drugs weren't necessary to alter one's consciousness. Bob, Lisa, Marie, I and some other friends met afterward for drinks.

Marie insisted that I sit next to her. She seemed genuinely glad to see me, though I was a bit uncomfortable knowing she came with someone else. I accepted an invitation from her to join her and some friends the next night. Her company was pleasant for the first time in six months. Marie's birthday was coming up soon and she agreed to have a date with me that night for a dinner being planned by Bob and Lisa. I hoped our relationship could be rekindled.

The next week I travelled to a Florida beach with someone else I was dating. The sun, sea, good food and her company gave me more pleasure than I had experienced since Brenda and I were in Australia. On the drive back to Atlanta, though, my friend wasn't feeling well. I made one of my controlling comments about what sort of hamburger she should buy, and though we laughed at the time, it was the beginning of the end of that short relationship with her.

The mercurial depressions of grief struck again during the days before Christmas. Once again I experienced the intense feelings of loss as I remembered Brenda and Grace. I had been trying to please new others since their deaths, without much success, and was just learning about pleasing myself, too.

Though it would be some days before I realized it, I had once again set myself up for depression by expecting others to like me in the same way I liked them. The reality was that they had other priorities ahead of me. I wasn't releasing those expectations that were inconsistent with reality, as I thought I had learned to do, so I became depressed again.

Expectations, reality, release. How easy it is for us to fool ourselves that reality is other than it is. True reality can be stated no more simply than a friend said after Brenda died, "*What is, is.*" It is a lesson I seem destined to repeat: the more you adjust your expectations to reality, the happier you will be. Preferring things to happen rather than expecting them to happen allows for more happiness. My attachment to unrealistic expectations set me up for unhappiness again.

The Christmas season had started on a high note. Buying a live Christmas tree was fun, and I hauled out the decorations Brenda and I had collected over the years, except a musical Santa she had loved. I still couldn't bear to hear its musical Christmas joy. I invited all my metaphysical friends over for an early December Christmas party to show off my decorations.

The group had grown - there were about 35 people this time. Both ladies in my life came, but one left alone early and Marie left with another man. Again I let the party run by itself, and all went smoothly from a functional standpoint, but that didn't stop me from being sad and lonely because both ladies I cared for did not reciprocate my feelings.

I felt abandoned, not to the degree I did when Brenda died, but left out nonetheless. With Christmas approaching, it wasn't easy for me to watch the new women in my life drifting further from me. I didn't know it at the time, but the double loss of both women caused my subconscious to shut down many of my feelings. Again loss, and its relentless companion, grief, pushed their way back into my life.

I began to feel utterly alone again, but in a different way. I felt a deep ache because I thought I needed someone important to me in my life. I was ready to risk a relationship, but the timing wasn't right. It would be several weeks before I was to understand why this was so.

As during the previous Christmas, I stayed busy virtually every night. One of those nights, I attended an SOS meeting, only my second one in all of 1985. My preoccupation with past life and metaphysical research, my compelling drive to date people and the belief that I "ought to" be over Brenda's death had kept me away from their non-judgmental support, which I felt I needed again during the holidays.

I spent Christmas with Bob, Lisa and Marie. Though they were very kind to me, I felt out of place. Later, I realized it was their Christmas, not mine, and vowed to have my own Christmas the next year, with or without a woman in my life.

That Christmas night, tired though she was, Lisa typed the following message from my guide Schuster. I had been debating that week whether to take a job with a long-time friend in his successful executive search firm. As usual, Schuster went right to the heart of my problems:

Jack, you are in no condition to take on the challenge of a new job right now. You have too much to clean up and clean out before you can go on with a new direction. You should give your all in a new venture and you just don't have it right now. The challenges will be there later. Don't feel that you have to jump on the bandwagon right now with this offer or any other offer that you may have in the next few months. You have more to go through in order to grow.

It's true, you have to take some shit, so to speak, in order to grow. You can intellectualize all you want, but you have to go through all of the feelings associated with relationships now and in the past, Brenda still included, before you can get a handle on what you will be doing with your future. Don't try to be including others in your future right now. It won't work. Think about yourself only and work on yourself only. Treasure your friends and friendships. They will be longer lasting than any permanent relationship that you try to pursue within the next few months.

You, like Lisa, need to release the past, come to terms with yourself and go forward. You're ready for nothing more right now than to relax, get in touch with yourself, let some anger and feelings out and have a good time. Damnit man, you don't allow yourself the pleasure of having fun! You start feeling guilty at the most inopportune times. Don't take it so serious, everything is coming as it should.

If you are looking for some income, look for something that is not confining or too complicated. If you want something that will keep you busy, take a look at your house and what repairs need to be done at this time, or new paint job, etc. You could make money with that house and you may want to take the next few months getting it ready to sell. Just a suggestion, but it would keep you occupied and it would help you release part of the past that you are holding on to without realizing it.

Listen to your intuition just like you have been doing and the rest will come easy. Stay in the flow. Don't get tied down to a job or one person. After the holidays it will be easier. I am around anytime you want to talk. Just close your eyes and I will be there. I will be whatever you want me to be, but I will be there. It is really good to communicate with you. Schuster.

What a wonderful Christmas present! Everything he said made sense, though I was again annoyed that I would have to continue waiting for the woman I longed for. After helping Bob and Lisa seal an opening where their storm window had blown in, shattering on the floor during the message from Schuster (that got my attention!), I headed towards my place from their Lake Lanier house.

Arriving home at the stroke of midnight, I felt the depression lifting. My reservations about returning to work had been supported by my guide, and I was finally willing to accept the reality of no relationship in my life. First, though, I had to make it through my birthday and New Year's Eve.

I couldn't help remembering the birthdays Brenda and I had shared, not anxious to broadcast adding another year to our lives. As so often happened then, thoughts of her intruded on my present moments.

The next day I began looking in depth at my relationships with women since Brenda had died. The women I had dated had several priorities higher than me, unlike Brenda who had placed me fairly high on her priority list. They felt children, jobs, other men, family and other friends usually came before me.

They hadn't come forth to help host the several parties I'd given, as I expected, because Brenda had been a charming hostess. Very few ever wanted to cuddle at my house, something Brenda and I loved to do. Recently, several of my favorite dates had opted for younger men, too.

After further reflection, I realized that I was deliberately dating extremely independent women. Brenda had been very dependent. I had overcompensated the other way since she had died, dating very strong, autonomous ladies who ran their own lives.

I decided to look for someone who would at least make me a priority in her life. I wanted to feel that occasionally I would even be the top priority in such a woman's world. The relationship that was coming did so, but only for awhile.

During my reflections, I retrieved from my files a wish list I had written five years earlier, after several months of therapy following Brenda's first suicide attempt. At the time, it pinpointed traits I wished Brenda showed more often. It read:

"I would like for my wife to be...

> A woman who enjoys giving and taking in a balanced way, who can do nice little things while graciously accepting my doing the same.

> A person who acts on her own, relying on my decisions in emergencies, large money matters, and other times when she chooses for me to decide (I no longer believe I am as chauvinistic as this one reads to me now).

A caring individual who knows I am important to her and who can frequently enjoy my happiness.

A companion who shares many of my interests, such as travel, work, games, house, pets, people, sex, politics, sports, kids and books.

A trim, attractive female who cares for herself, physically and mentally, through exercise, nutrition, and judicious use of drugs, doctors, stimulants, and advice from others.

A realistically oriented person who strives to be grateful for what she has.

A responsive lover who can vocalize her passion, allows her body to respond with movement, & can occasionally initiate new forms of lovemaking.

A friend I can talk to about my good days and bad, who listens with an uncritical ear, and who expects the same from me.

A woman who realizes my weaknesses and gently helps me overcome them, reduce them or ignore them.

An adult who knows romance often comes from simple and frequently unexpected sources.

A sensitive person who lives with a genuine feeling of good will toward others.

A persistent woman who knows what she wants and is strongly committed to achieve those wants.

A fairly practical person well aware of her own and others' strengths and limitations, including the sure knowledge that she could not provide all of the above, and that I do not expect all of the above."

Though I now felt far less picky than I had been five years earlier, and now knew more about reality, nevertheless I believed there were women that had many of the qualities I was looking for. My goal for 1986 would be to make sure I attracted women with the traits I wanted. Without knowing it, I was creating the reality I desired in that coming year by visualizing the woman I longed for in my life. However, as I would learn later, I left out several very important qualities, such as gentleness, loyalty, courtesy, interest in my world and physical compatibility.

With my outline of the ideal woman very much on my mind I said goodbye to 1985 at a small party hosted by some old friends. I was determined to get my own internal house in order for the new and better year.

Chapter 8

The New Me Begins

January - July, 1986

In this new year I really wanted to explore more of my feeling, intuitive, loving side, the feminine side of my brain (often called the right brain). This feeling side of me had been suppressed for years, and I needed to release more of my pent-up emotions and learn to better deal with feelings. I was increasingly aware that learning to express my emotions is a primary reason for being here.

My days after the holidays were depressing. I was besieged by the nagging "shoulds" and "ought to's" that had plagued my life. "I ought to be over Brenda by now," I thought. "I ought to be working again. I should have a significant woman in my life by now." I even thought "I should develop my feminine energy to become aware of and release my negative feelings." Since there was no one in particular I wanted to date, I went into virtual seclusion. In truth, I was really "dating" me, so to speak.

As I worked at getting in touch with my feelings, the first ones to surface were angry. I couldn't pinpoint the source of the anger until Jackie said that a great deal of my anger centered around trying to live by others' rules when they themselves didn't follow those rules. She suggested I start living by my rules.

I had tried most of my life to please other people, only to find the more I tried to please, the less satisfied they and I were. It was a vicious circle; they expected certain behavior from me and I in turn expected they would be grateful. Attempts to live up to the expectations of others would probably only lead me to more anger and misery, though it would be a long time before I addressed these codependent traits.

I thought I was doing the right thing by appeasing rather than getting mad. Because I had spent so much time trying to please and appease everyone besides me, I had developed the bad habit of manipulating people. Manipulation is an indirect, passive-aggressive and usually self-defeating way of coping with the world that says, in essence, I won't get mad, but I will get even. Also, guilt is frequently used as a lever to have people do what is wanted of them.

I had developed a compulsive, controlling, judgmental way of living my life. I was seeing and trying to control reality only with my logical left brain. Psychologists, books, friends, psychics and my guides had been pointing these tendencies out for a long time, but I hadn't been very receptive.

Now I was less resistant to change, for my new life without Brenda included frequent changes. My left brain knew that happiness can only come from within. Now it was time for me to program my right brain with the same message.

To start with, on those lonely winter days, I began taking each day as it was, without expectations. On each day I allowed whatever feelings were in me to flow. This led to a major relapse into grief. I cried and cursed a lot during those weeks. I was angry that suicide was so different from divorce. At least with divorce there is some hope of reconciliation, but death ends any physical reconciliation.

I began to wonder, "Will my grief ever end? Would I ever be able to change my outlook on life and make it stick permanently? Would I ever have a loving relationship with a woman again?" Fortunately, Jackie said she used to be very like me in her perception of the world, and she had changed. She assured me I could, too. I hoped so, with her and others' help.

The weather that January was warmer and sunnier than normal, so I replanted some bushes outside the house. As always, digging in the earth calmed and centered me. And, for the first time in my life, I grew a beard, just for the heck of it. My old logical self fought this decision, telling me my friends and family might not approve, particularly anyone I wanted to date. The new me won, though, and I stopped shaving. I would risk the possible disapproval of others.

The few people I saw during the early weeks of growing the beard didn't seem to mind my scruffy appearance; in fact, quite a few thought I looked good with a beard. I couldn't wait to surprise my other friends with my new look.

Though often lonely, angry and depressed, I don't think I've ever felt as free as I did then. My brother and his wife were in the Bahamas, my mother was in South America, and I had no relationship with a woman. There was no job, no land to sell, and I had money in the bank. What a wonderful opportunity to go within, to work on and play with me!

I tried forgiving people: my wife for leaving this life and abandoning me, my mother for her ways of behaving, my relationships that hadn't worked out and myself for just being human. I thought "If we came into this life to learn, how could we do so without making mistakes?" I wasn't perfect, and I had the painful memories to prove it.

As they say in football, I had played much of my life in pain. It was time for me to grow away from playing in pain toward playing with joy. Too much of my pain was self-inflicted from allowing guilt, anger and fear to dictate my actions, rather than accepting myself lovingly and enjoying the moment. I would for awhile ease up on Jack and stop judging him.

In early February I heard a talk by a new teacher in town. The talk was sponsored by a group I had heard of but had not joined because it didn't feel right to me. In retrospect, I could have saved myself a lot of pain had I heeded that earlier feeling. However, I felt that speech would give me an opportunity to get out and to meet more people interested in personal development.

I immediately liked this teacher named John Harricharan, feeling that I had known him from somewhere. That day, he had learned his wife had cancer, yet he went on to teach others that night. "What courage and strength of spirit," I thought, "to go on stage in the face of such devastating news."

That night I saw his aura, a pale lime-yellow glow around his head. I had heard a lot about auras, something all of us are said to have. At first I thought I was imagining what I saw, until the lady next to me commented on his lime-yellow aura. Was I becoming more psychic? Was my right brain finally beginning to function as I wanted it to? I hoped so.

After his talk several of us met for drinks. "Now there's a lady I could date," I thought, looking at the woman sitting next to me, whom I'll call Sandy. She was attractive, trim, businesslike, and bright. She worked during the week for a large corporation. "Too bad she seems to be involved with the director of the group," I thought. Little did I know she had recently composed a list in an effort to find her ideal man. I found out later that the list was remarkably detailed and extraordinarily close to a description of me.

We both presumed the other was in a relation-ship. I had no way of knowing then this woman soon would be in my life for the next two and a half years, the most significant relationship by far since Brenda died.

I returned to my house late that evening, trying to decide what to do with the rest of my life. In the days that followed I went on some half-hearted computer sales job interviews, worked on this book and planted some more roses. For the first time since Brenda died, I was not consciously seeking a relationship with another woman, not compulsively searching for someone else to be the center of my life.

I felt more secure being independent, rather than seeking feelings of security through the approval of others. I was becoming more comfortable being on my own, without a significant other in my life. In fact, I had come to know that having people around me extracted a price I was just beginning to understand.

I have always been extremely sensitive to other people's emotions. I had learned this may be a psychic ability called clairsentience, which is the ability to sense feelings in others. I had avoided emotion-filled events and places such as weddings, funerals, hospi-tals and arguments most of my life, perhaps because the emotions broadcast in those situations were just too overwhelming for me.

To help me cope with this ability, several people taught me a technique called "shielding" that made it much easier for me to be around intensely emotional people. I imagine myself surrounded by a large bubble and visualize strong emotions bouncing off this bubble into space. Naming the whole visualization process "shield," all I have to do is say the word in my mind and my subconscious recreates the bubble, stopping the emotional bombardment almost instantly.

But, I didn't need to use this new technique too often then, since I wasn't around people much of the time. I looked forward to spring and a life with fewer expectations, less complications, and greater distance in time from my loss.

My beard was beginning to make me feel and look like an author and this inspired me. I found placing the words on paper forced me to relive the past year and a half and release some of the stored emotions from my loss. Though the writing required hard work at a time when I was enjoying being relaxed, I stayed with a discipline that usually found me writing at least four hours a day.

Late in March I decided to attend a party sponsored by the group I mentioned earlier. I wanted to see some friends at the party and hoped Sandy might be there without a date. My pendulum said we hadn't shared previous lives together and we weren't soulmates, but I was definitely drawn to her. Earlier in the month we had talked on the phone about the group and my ideas for it.

My intuition was right, for she came by herself. As the party broke up, she suggested some of us go dancing. There were no takers besides me, so we decided instead to go to my house for a drink and conversation. We talked comfortably for a long time. She enjoyed my rubbing her stiff back, which stirred me in a way I hadn't felt for quite a while.

We seemed from the beginning to be good friends. I thought a lot that night and in the days and weeks to follow how much she matched my own list of what I wanted in a woman.

As I had envisioned years earlier, she enjoyed giving and taking, though that would change. She had been single for 10 years, so she could obviously act on her own and seemed realistic. We shared many of the same interests, and she was trim and very attractive.

I found her to be a very responsive friend I could talk with easily. Practical, apparently honest, seemingly sensitive, and persistent as a bulldog further described her from my wish list of 1980.

We began to see each other every weekend and often during the week. Her son had activities away from her during those first weekends, giving us a better opportunity to get to know each other.

The spring months were filled with fun and contentment for me. I didn't find myself head over heels in love with Sandy, but felt wonderfully at ease around her. We found more and more in common as the weeks flew by. It appeared then that she had few expectations of me, preferring to just be with me.

Her birthday was just three days before Brenda's, making Sandy also a Taurus. This second anniversary of not celebrating Brenda's birthday was less painful, as I made it through the day much more easily.

Late April brought an old friend from computer sales back into my life. He, too, had grown a beard, so we enjoyed comparing notes on this new phenomenon for us. He casually mentioned that he might have an opening in Atlanta for me, but I wasn't really interested. Prophetically, I did decide then that if I were to return to the highly competitive computer sales world, it would take an offer of $50,000 guaranteed, to lure me out of my prolonged vacation.

I later attended a seminar conducted by John Harricharan and his friend, Brad Steiger, who had written the introduction to John's thought-provoking book, When You Can Walk On Water, Take The Boat. Brad's own books had meant a great deal to me, particularly during my reincarnation studies, and I found him to be a delightfully warm and wise man.

That night I hosted another party at my house for my metaphysical friends. Sandy enjoyed meeting many of them for the first time, and their feedback to me appeared positive about her. I reminisced that night about how lucky I was to have my new supportive lady with me.

Relationship problems didn't seem to exist for me during May, perhaps because she and I were so new to each other and because my own feelings for her had not yet deepened. Was I finally rid of my old problem with female relationships in May?

In reality, I believe I was repeating my old pattern of trying hard to please Sandy. I went out of my way to fit into her world. I was determined to make this relationship last, at all costs. I began submerging my own needs and wants and let her control me, which is a strong codependent trait.

My appearance was an area I still controlled, though. I showed up one afternoon at her apartment without my beard. Perhaps it was becoming too hot for a beard in the summer or maybe I was subconsciously preparing to re-enter the corporate computer world. This may have been a passive-aggressive way of showing the anger that was building over my trying to conform to her world.

Sandy was truly shocked at my clean-shaven appearance. She and her family had only known me wearing a beard, so the change in appearance was dramatic for them, in some ways a loss of identity for both me and them. I had not shared with her my decision and she was hurt, though we continued as if nothing had happened.

In late June we went to hear a medical doctor from California talk about crystals he had used with his patients to help them heal. He was listening to a musical tape called The Fairy Ring by Mike Rowland as we walked in. I had never heard anything so relaxing in my life. Sandy had already introduced me to this gentle style of music, so I bought the tape for us. Thus began a new hobby for me, that of listening to the soft strains of this new generation of relaxation music.

My attraction for this exquisitely beautiful tape was symbolic of a more relaxed me during the summer of 1986, in spite of my return to the old habits of trying to please others and take care of them.

I felt reasonably contented for one of the rare times in my life. I went along with my new lady's plans most of the time, telling myself that my schedule was far more flexible than hers, since I had no job. In addition to contentment, I may also have found that returning to an old codependent behavior pattern felt better to me for awhile.

On the second July anniversary of Brenda's death, Sandy stayed with me that night to be sure I was all right. She watched my anxiety increase as the hour of Brenda's death two years earlier approached. I showed her pictures of us. She sensed that I was reaching out for Brenda in my mind and heart. Perhaps I was pre-occupied, because I have no recollection of showing the pictures or crying any tears.

This second anniversary seemed much easier than the year before. The day itself didn't have the impact of the previous year, either, until the evening hours. Perhaps the advice was true, that distance from my loss would make anniversaries less painful. More likely, though, I was again being codependent by suppressing honest emotions and putting on a happy face.

Chapter 9

Months Turn To Years

August, 1986 - June, 1989

Though filled with discoveries and learning, those first two years after Brenda died were the toughest years of my life. I thought earlier that nothing could match the stress of my two jobs, her son's problems, her multiple ailments, my own growth problems, and my turning forty, but I was wrong. Those previous stresses seem insignificant after surviving Brenda's suicide.

The days of survival had turned to weeks and the weeks turned to months. Finally, the months had turned to years, and the pain was fading. In my attempt to "be over" Brenda's death, I postponed my final grief work as I poured myself into my new relationship and her world for several years.

My friend and bearded former co-worker called to see if I would consider selling computers again. "No, I wasn't really interested," I said, but I looked forward to seeing him the next time he was in town.

He phoned a few days later and dangled the very $50,000 figure I had imagined in May.

I accepted the position, because I could use the money, I liked and respected him and I wanted to prove that I could work in the regular world again. Besides, I had said to myself I would take such a job if it were offered, and here it was, just as I had said it had to be.

Thus, another striking example of visualizing what I wanted and waiting for it to show up had occurred in my life, similar to the visualized new relationship with Sandy that had begun earlier in the year. Visualization works, so be very careful of what you see coming - it may happen.

My relationship with Sandy went well for the first six months as we had fun together. We found we had a great deal in common. She was ready for commitment, though, and I wasn't. My two failed relationships plus unfinished grief work over Brenda left me very wary of any firm commitment on my part. I think I had turned off my feelings again in my attempt to avoid hurt.

At the end of about six months, as Dr. M. Scott Peck says in The Road Less Travelled, the romantic love of my new relationship began to fade in favor of reality. It became very obvious to me that her realities were quite different from mine, but I chose to deny that knowledge in favor of trying to force both the personal and business relationships to work.

I ignored many of my psychic friends who saw the relationship ending. I might also have heeded the common folk wisdom of not mixing business with pleasure, including loaning money. I worked hard in her business without pay, and overlooked too frequently her tendency to let ends justify the means.

I would spend the next two years trying to become what she wanted, though never to her satisfaction. Unfortunately, because our realities were so different, we saw the world through very different perspectives. My codependent nature would not let go of her, so she ended the relationship by bringing another man into her personal and business life.

I had just become aware of codependent behavior when we parted late in 1988, so I devoted myself to the study of this emotionally crippling condition. I went to several Codependents Anonymous (CoDA) meetings and read every book I could find on the subject. I also renewed my interest in its usual side effect, passive-aggressive behavior.

Brenda was addicted to alcohol and perhaps prescription drugs. And she had another habit, one many of us share, that of compulsively fixing other people, now called codependency. Friends would often call to ask her advice. She would become embroiled in their problems, taking them on as her own.

Sandy seemed to be habitually compelled to work and to have relationships, both of which are codependent traits. I understand work addiction, since I have been a workaholic. Brenda used to ask me to "please sit down and rest once in awhile" as I compulsively did things around the house after coming home from work. I occasionally relapse into workaholism even now, and I certainly understand the compulsion to be in a relationship.

My life with Julia, Brenda and Sandy was constantly disrupted by their habitual behavior, which I allowed and even encouraged with my own codependent behavior. As those of you know who have lived with addiction, those habits drive all lives in the household.

When the relationship with Sandy ended, I bottomed out over my own addiction to relationships. I no longer wanted to be trapped by my need for someone, or behave in ways that drove them away. The time had finally come for me to address this self-defeating behavior and come to terms with it at last.

What is codependent behavior? In my case, I assumed too much responsibility for Brenda's and others' feelings and behavior, while at the same time being unable to identify my own feelings. When asked how I felt, I really didn't know, so usually I'd just say I was fine. I remember Brenda, Marie, and Sandy often asking what I really thought or felt. I really didn't know! This is also a classic symptom of passive-aggressive behavior, which I believe is intimately interwoven with codependence.

I was afraid of how others would respond if I showed my real feelings, with a particularly strong fear of being hurt and rejected by others. So, I would modify my behavior to coincide with other people's actions and beliefs, saying what I thought they wanted to hear. In fact, their wants and needs always came before my own. I could never do anything well enough, mainly because I would try to live up to another codependent's high expectations.

Most people in our society are addicted to relationships, work, sex, gambling, religion, or even support groups; or they are hooked on substances such as alcohol, narcotics, food, or cigarettes. They too, are codependent. In other words, most addictive people are codependent.

Relationships between codependents, which most of mine have been, seem to be the most explosive of all. Both parties try to please and appease the other, stuffing anger and resentment until these emotions explode, often as a raging, out-of-control temper tantrum.

That's what would happen with Brenda. We would lose control and scream at each other, with her often hurling dishes around the room and me sometimes storming out of the house. Two such rage explosions occurred with Sandy, the second of which precipitated the end of the affair and pointedly showed me that my own codependence was an affliction I must deal with.

Some codependent tendencies can be very positive. One such trait is staunch loyalty, if practiced with appropriate people. Unfortunately, we usually display this steadfastness with addictive people who abuse it. This often unwarranted loyalty lasted far past the end of all my relationships.

Another positive trait of codependents is that we really care about other people, usually to our own detriment. Several years after Brenda died, I wound up loaning money to several friends. Many of them are not friends any longer (perhaps they never were) because of problems that developed due to the loan. I think they had a real need, but when I helped them fill that need through overly caring (cartetaking), they wound up resenting me.

Codependence is mostly negative, though. I think it's a harder addiction to break than substance addiction. I know quitting cigarettes was a "piece of cake" for me compared to ending my compulsive need to help people. I've heard many substance abusers at CoDA meetings verify that breaking their substance addiction has proven far less difficult than breaking their compulsive codependent need for a relationship.

Where do you turn for help? Fortunately, now there are hundreds of CoDA groups around the country. At these groups I found I could share my experiences with other people fixers, most of whom had a string of unsatisfactory relationships like mine.

As with deep grief, I also suggest counseling for this affliction. If you think you might be codependent, professional help for awhile may be needed. I also needed help dealing with grief over the realization of how much damage my codependence had done to those closest to me.

Further, I read every book I could find dealing with codependence. They included Melody Beattie's Codependent No More, Anne Wilson Schaef's When Society Becomes an Addict, Dr. Charles L. Whitfield's Healing the Child Within, Earnie Larsen's Stage II Relationships - Love Beyond Addiction, and Janet G. Woititz's Struggle for Intimacy. If you find yourself among the estimated 95% of the population who are codependent, these books may help you as they helped me.

As I mourned the loss of my most recent love, I experienced again all the strong emotions of deep grief as I learned anew living without a love companion. The loneliness returned with a vengeance. I had deluded myself again into thinking a woman I loved would change if I just did enough for her. We both had expectations the other could not meet.

Here I was, now 47-years-old and starting over again. In looking back, it seemed I had learned nothing from my previous failed relationships, since I had made many of the same mistakes again. But this time I knew what I had failed to do and have taken steps to change.

I did learn from Sandy. I saw a woman who could work hard towards her goal. We did keep the relationship going for two and a half years. In the beginning, she showed me that I was loveable, which I had begun to doubt. Near the end, she made me aware that I needed to define my own goals.

The breakup allowed me to spend time with my mother in Florida as she sympathetically listened to my sad tale. As the friend she has become, she provided wise and sure counsel to ease my emotional pain. We even decided to take a two-month trip to the South Seas that would almost duplicate Brenda's and my trip of five years earlier.

Those times spent with my mother convinced me that she had either changed miraculously over the past few years, or I had. We had become more like equals, with each valuing the other's opinion. Our travels together were pleasant and rewarding. I particularly enjoyed her intuitive flashes and her more generous and open way of looking at the world.

The South Seas trip found me missing Sandy more than Brenda. During the trip, I realized that most of my remaining grief over losing Brenda had been washed out by the tears shed over the end of my latest relationship.

I cried much longer and harder over this new loss than I had over Brenda, though some of the tears were overdue emotions finally releasing from the loss of my wife. I believe that I allowed the grief to flow this time more fully, allowing me to get on with my life sooner than if I resisted my feelings of loss.

During the trip to Florida with my mother, a very spiritual event gave me hope for the future. It was a bright, brisk day, with a cloudless sky floating over a calm Gulf of Mexico as the tide neared its high mark. As I walked along the beach I spotted a dolphin swimming along the shore towards me. I had never seen a lone dolphin before. This one turned around as our paths came closest and began to follow me down the beach.

Occasionally it would dart to and fro searching for a tasty fish or two, coming as close as 10 feet away, so close I could hear its breathing. Soon I discovered I could see it below the murky water if I looked for its light-colored lower half. Sometimes I would stop to let it catch up, like waiting for a dog that must sniff each bush during a walk.

I had decided to turn around and head back when the dolphin dashed for the shore, nearly beaching itself as it splashed a wave at my feet. It then swam back down the beach, apparently sensing that I was ready to head back. I smiled for the first time in several weeks.

Once again it would fall behind, but now I listened for its puff of air to gauge how far back it was. Out in the Gulf, a fishing trawler motored along with a swarm of seagulls following it, looking for food too small for the nets. But my dolphin was oblivious to all this, content to stay near me.

I noticed from its size and slightly tattered dorsal fin that it was an older dolphin. "What message was it bringing me?" I wondered. Suddenly I realized it was saying "I'm doing fine all by myself. I might rather be with my friends and have a mate, but I'm OK as I am."

As we approached a teenage boy and girl kissing on the beach, the dolphin turned out to sea, staying on the surface as if to wave goodbye with its fin. Perhaps the young people and the special dolphin were symbolic indications that romance would again be mine someday.

Chapter 10

Lessons

My long, five-year soul journey from Brenda's death has brought much of the learning and growing that the long ago voice in my head told me was coming. I have learned enough to realize I really know so little. And, I sometimes wish the lessons could have been gentler.

Finding Brenda dead that night shattered my confidence as well as my world, for I felt worthless and I even hated myself. Such emotions create a challenge for those who are left behind after suicide. Though few of us survivors could commit suicide because we know the devastating pain of being left behind, we do struggle with feeling good about ourselves.

It is the climb back to a healthy self-esteem that became one of my greatest tasks as a survivor, and returned as a hurdle when my long term relationship ended. In rebuilding my self-worth I rediscovered a secret of happiness; *I did the best I could with what I knew at the time.* I've understood this truth for years and now I live it most of the time.

After my long term relationship with Sandy ended, I refused to let my old need for a companion overwhelm me, choosing to not attempt a relationship until my self-esteem was stronger. Though feeling good about being me was slow in coming, I finally became glad to be on my own, with few unchosen responsibilities.

I'm healing my codependent tendencies and finding the positive, happy Jack that has occasionally surfaced in the past. I don't require a woman's validation to find that happiness.

I am stronger and more sure of myself than before. I am trying to develop the character to say what I believe, rather than going along with the crowd as I have so often done. I'm not as afraid of emotional honesty and commitment as I used to be.

You see, I've learned I can survive alone. For a long time I thought I couldn't, and my addiction to relationships has brought women in and out of my life. But often for many months I would be alone, and I came to enjoy those alone times. Besides, I had friends and other supporters who contributed so much to my recovery.

How did I make it through the grief? In a word, *support*. The deepest and most consistent support I received was from friends, old and new. From my wonderful neighbors that first night to the many kind souls who helped me later, I seemed to be blessed with loving, nurturing friends. Those new friends who appeared in the months after Brenda died were perhaps heeding my subconscious call for help.

Most friends were compassionate, supportive and as helpful as they could be. They invited me over for dinner in the early days, took care of details I couldn't address during my depressions and shored up my weak self-image for years after her death.

The experience of overwhelming loss reveals who your real friends are. Some friends couldn't seem to handle the grief, so I didn't see much of them. Sometimes their lack of support hurt, but I now know their absence was the best way, for them, of "handling" their own grief over Brenda's death.

I use the word friends in the broader sense. That is, many people who care for me and me for them, even though we may not be together often and may not share all of our secrets. In the narrower sense, typically there are only a very few friends who know most of my intimate secrets. Those very close few would tell me the truth and were there all along, giving of themselves freely.

Some of my new friends came from the more formalized support groups such as Al-Anon, SOS, and CoDA. At these groups, I received support in specific areas, and from all a compassionate understanding of what I had been through. Each group had experienced some of what I had gone through, and, being anonymous groups, would not repeat the thoughts and feelings I shared.

I had to give myself permission to accept support. The staunch independent image I had of myself had to be discarded for a new, inter-dependent person who needed the feedback and nurturing of other people. Without them, I do not know what I would be like today, but I couldn't have grown this much alone.

My grief recovery included many old and new hobbies, which helped me keep my sanity. Before she died, Brenda used to kid me about moving plants around, for I had subconsciously discovered that digging in the earth helped balance me and reduce my stress.

She had given me a calligraphy print which said "When the world wearies and society ceases to satisfy there is always the garden." (Aumonier). The year after Brenda died, and the times after my several failed relationships, certainly bore out Aumonier's wisdom. I could always retreat to my flower bushes, which never expected anything from me and didn't ask me to change for their pleasure. They don't argue and they don't abuse my normally good will.

When the pain became too great or anger or depression gripped my soul, I could always find something to do in the yard that put my past away from view and put worries about my future aside. I always came in from a few hours in the yard less wracked with emotional pain and pleasantly sore physically. I always feel that I've accomplished something after working in the yard.

If I felt like it, I would take long walks. My mood always improved after them, particularly if tears came along the way. Sitting around, often wallowing in self-pity, there were many days that I didn't walk. I wish someone had booted me out of the house at those times, for now I know the walks would have helped immensely.

I also love to read. Many, many hours have I spent curled up with a good book. After devouring, through my tears, the last books Brenda read, I read about life after death, then zeroed in on reincarnation, including my own past life research. This diversion lasted many months and filled countless hours that otherwise might have become intolerably lonely.

There were very few books about the grief process early in my recovery from losing her, though recently many very good ones have been written. I did read what was available, and became more knowledgeable about the process, as I said in Chapter 4. I hope my knowledge of the grieving process will help me and others through future times of loss.

Dyer's book The Sky's The Limit had shown me I needed to make some changes. I began to realize after Brenda's death how out of touch I was with my own emotions. I read a lot about love, anger, depression, assertiveness, passive aggression, and more recently, the books on addiction and codependence. These have all helped me deal with my feelings.

I spent some of my recovery as a so-called "couch potato," watching television when I was depressed, much as Brenda had done for many of her days. I now believe that such mindless time was necessary for me and see nothing wrong with doing so, provided such escape doesn't last for years or serve as denial of the grief process by blocking normal mourning emotions.

I found myself far more emotional over some of the shows, much as Brenda had been. I used to laugh at her for being so mushy, but now I know from experience why she cried so often during movies. They often trigger memories in me that need more emotional release, as they may have for her.

My love of music led me into the world of relaxation music. I began collecting low-key meditative music and eventually went on to write reviews of such music for various publications. This has been one of my most enjoyable pastimes and has actually produced some income. My love of reading has also led to writing book reviews.

I attended a host of workshops and talks about human development. These provided insights into my own growth needs, and perhaps most importantly, kept my mind and emotions off of my losses for awhile. Some were conducted by my counselors, others were of interest at the time. These dealt with many areas of human potential, often using metaphysical or parapsychological concepts. The most consistent and practical teacher I found to be Lazaris, whose wisdom put me in touch again with spirituality.

Lazaris suggests that spirituality need be nothing more complicated than being honest, happy, expressing emotions, handling imperfections and not intentionally hurting others. I had encountered the need for spirituality in Peck's The Road Less Travelled, right after Brenda's death, not yet knowing consciously that I was beginning my own spiritual awakening.

I know for me that finding a spiritual path was one of the great lessons from Brenda's death. I believe spirituality is a very personal issue, and whatever religion or creed feels right for each of us is fine. I don't believe attendance is mandatory at a church, synagogue, or mosque to grow spiritually, though those sacred centers can certainly aid growth for some.

I found my own path back toward God only after I lost my beloved. I'm told it doesn't have to be so, but most of us seem to need pain first before we choose to grow. And often that choice to grow will include a relationship with our higher power.

I found that the teachings of behavioral psychology, metaphysics and spirituality had a common thread. They all seemed to be saying: *"Get in touch with your emotions, for that is the secret of happiness."* The hardest part of my recovery was finding my true feelings and the most difficult part of this book has been the attempt to record on paper these emotions.

How do you describe hurt, anguish, guilt or despair? What words do you use to paint a picture of loneliness, confusion, doubt or anxiety? Because of my background, I was very out of touch with my emotional self, thus I first had to learn to feel any emotion fully before trying to describe it. Often I re-experienced loss before those emotions would finally surface.

My friends have watched me over the past five years as I struggled to let my feelings flow. Slowly, oh so slowly, my defenses have fallen away and more of my feelings began to show, first as a seepage and then as a flow, with an occasional tidal wave thrown in. The emotional outbursts weren't always pretty, or am I particularly proud of the way some were vented, but they needed to come out from behind the blocks that held them in.

I believe there are two basic emotions, love and fear, from which all other feelings are derived. It is fear that lies behind all the negative and debilitating emotions we experience, for instance, during deep grief. I believe these must be experienced to be able to feel more love.

I was told early in my healing that there are no right or wrong emotions, that feelings just "are." The negative emotions are valid and must be expressed to enjoy the positive emotions more fully. The key is expression, not suppression. I'll say it again - *there are no wrong emotions,* a key lesson for me.

We all have fears, and I have my fair share of them. Acknowledging these and dealing with them became one of my biggest challenges. Many of those fears erupted into view after Brenda died and again when relationships crumbled.

A fear of commitment has gripped me since her death. I don't want to lose my precious freedom and I'm leery of being hurt again. So, like many codependents, part of me shied away from commitment while another part longed for someone to commit to me.

Another fear that has dominated my life has been my fear of abandonment. Like most human beings, I don't like the prospect of always being alone. I have tended to stay in codependent relationships that aren't working, driven by this dread of being left alone.

The twin fears of commitment and abandonment have ruled my relationships, a reign I am working very hard at ending. The two fears feed on each other, ruining true intimacy. Those fears have kept me distant from, yet possessive of, the women in my life.

Then there is the fear of the unknown. Even though Brenda had her share of problems, as did our relationship, at least our marriage was a known quantity. Taking risks as new relationships develop is scary, even for the boldest among us. However, each time I now turn "unknown" into "known" I feel a sense of triumph.

Perhaps the most universal fear for me was that of death, an unknown that has become almost a known for me. I am convinced that we live on after our bodies die. I'm sometimes concerned about the ways of dying, particularly the painful ones, but I know my spirit will live on. This knowledge has proven invaluable for me as I face other losses and as I grow older.

I still suppress my anger around other people more than I would like. As much as I have learned, this society we live in doesn't want to put up with anger, so we are constantly encouraged to deny it. Suppressed anger is the basis of the codependence and the passive aggression that often characterized me, many of my relationships and most of our society.

But here are some ways I cope with it, to express the anger away from people. One method is to write a letter telling all your emotions, but refrain from sending it. Of course, I have sometimes sent them, to my later regret. Another way of venting anger is to frequently walk around the house screaming, though your neighbors might wonder about your sanity.

Then there is the trick of beating the pillow. Blows rained on a pillow hurt no one and can release pent-up feelings. Or you might try telling a trusted and close friend or counselor of your emotions, particularly anger. I'll use whatever technique I can to vent my anger, because I've seen what denying it does to me and others I have loved.

Spontaneous joy has been too rare for me in the past. Much of that lack stemmed from living in the past or future rather than in the now. As I live more and more in the moment, I feel my capacity for joy increasing daily, so it is a lesson still being learned.

I'm also working on creating more serenity. That feeling of peace and tranquility happens more often now. I experience this inner peace when I meditate, but maintaining serenity, too, is a lesson I'm still learning.

I need laughter in my life. I know when I don't laugh at me that I'm under stress. As I find the other positive emotions I seek, more laughter enters my life.

I want more time to be, just to be, and to spend less time doing. I realize most of my life has been spent doing (called by Lazaris the masculine energy). I used to stay busy to avoid feelings or getting to know me better.

I had never really thought much about just being. I have structured my life more towards this new way of being (identified as the feminine energy by Lazaris), since being seems to mean allowing the universe to respond to my needs.

I play more now than I used to. That means I'm more spontaneous and more likely to change plans quickly. I look for friends who enjoy what I enjoy and spend time with them. As part of my campaign to become more childlike again, I let my curiosity drive me.

145

Healthy children can teach us so much. Their honesty, openness, curiosity and sense of joy and wonder are traits I want more of. Children live naturally in the now until taught by adults to worry about tomorrow or to regret past actions.

I definitely have improved my ability to live in the present moment. The message from Wayne Dyer and many others has finally penetrated my tendency to regret the past and worry about the future. I find myself more content with the present moment.

My compulsive need for neatness and order seems to have lessened since my tragedy. In the past, dishes piled in the sink or a messy desk would have required my immediate attention. Now, dishes stay in the sink for many days unwashed and my desk is the tangled mass of papers more typical of my expressive personality. My refrigerator is littered with positive messages now.

Why did I need to be right so often in the past? Was it because I thought I was better than or less than others? Was it a need to judge them? Did they really influence my life that much, or was I truly responsible for my own life? I don't have to be right as much anymore, except for me.

I'm more forgiving of my own faults and am trying to be more forgiving of other's flaws. I'm more discerning about who I call friends, while attempting to resist judgment of those who are not friends, though I have much to learn in the area of judgment.

Another lesson I continue to learn is to not take myself or what happens to me too seriously. Codependents tend to do that, as do those who choose to improve themselves. Now I don't spend as much time analyzing what happened and why, instead I enjoy the reality of right now.

I am more inclined to let things happen as they will, rather than trying to be in control, though I'm still growing in this area. I hope I have learned the difference between letting others control my life, which I no longer choose to do, and letting events control themselves without my trying to take charge of them. The Al-Anon saying of "Let go and let God" has begun to take real effect in my life.

I am learning to deal with my own codependency, for if I don't, I will continue to attract addictive people that I may feel compelled to fix. I have added to my list of ideals for my wife. What I want now is a life mate who can balance work and play, who can share in my dreams as I share in hers. I need someone with gentleness to match my own and who will be loyal through tough times.

I'll leave to God the timing of such a person in my life, though my support system is well aware that I'm receptive. I am not as afraid of commitment to her now as I had been since Brenda died. The new skills I've worked on make me want to use them to deepen a relationship.

Those skills have deepened my relationship with Mom into a friendly acknowledgment of each other's right to live our lives as we choose. We talk at least once a week, because I want to, not because I have to. This new acceptance of my mother is one of the treasures that came to me as a result of Brenda's death.

Iris had said in that first SOS meeting in 1984 that there might be an unexpected gift from Brenda's death. Along with the new friendship with my mother, I had found the gift of spirituality, including my now strong belief in eternal life.

Then there is the gift of knowing more about my strengths and weaknesses now, and feeling far more comfortable with both. I am more content with the present, more honest with myself, more accepting of others, and perhaps more loving. I look forward to learning and growing always.

As in all learning, you must decide for yourself whether to choose bitterness over your losses or to see losses as lessons, as a challenge to your own spiritual growth.

Chapter 11

Brenda & Me Revisited

This has been a book that began with two people who became separated when one deliberately died and the other chose to survive. It's the story about my learning and growth after our physical separation, and my recovery from that enormous loss. I hope, in whatever reality her spirit lives now, that she has done the same.

From the overwhelming despair of finding Brenda dead nearly five years ago, I now find life more exhilarating and far less stressful. You may think my experiences bizarre and incredible, and that's fine, because I think some of them were bizarre and incredible, too.

The Jack Clarke of five years ago would certainly consider that the current edition of Jack had completely lost his mind. Believe in psychics? Soulmates? Make pendulums swing without moving my hand? Past lives? See auras? Automatic writing? Spirit possession? "Be real, that's all hogwash," would have been my response.

What about visualizing what you want and it occurs? Helping others without thought of any return? Not demanding that people live up to my expectations? Getting what I want by asking for it, rather than manipulating? Expressing my feelings openly? "That's not me," the previous edition of me would have said.

But that Jack hadn't lost the center of his life yet. His wife had not killed herself. He had yet to wade through the roller coaster grief emotions, to have to search for a new center for his life. He was duty-driven, not love-driven. He had no idea of the power the soul has at its disposal, that higher power available to us all.

Does the new Jack really believe in reincarnation? I think it's quite probable, though many explanations are possible for the thousands of case histories I've studied. I also think that Christians and Jews once believed in this concept, but early church leaders decided differently.

I've concluded that my instant attraction to some of the new people, who came into my life after Brenda died, came from earlier lives with them. It's very difficult to learn all the lessons we need to in one life. I believe this planet is a good classroom, so we keep coming back until we have learned our lessons.

What about soulmates? I think we have many soulmates, with different levels of comfort together. However, I believe we develop into soulmates at some time together. If so, why look forever for soulmates when you could become one with anyone you choose to? Why not start now with someone who is already in your life?

Do I believe in psychic ability? Absolutely. I've begun to have psychic experiences myself, and have seen too many demonstrations of this capability we all have. Watching my friend become an automatic writer was proof in itself for me. I don't advocate letting some psychic run your life, however, because a person can change the future by their thoughts and actions. I have done so several times already, and I'm still new at this.

Can we see auras? Yes, if we want to. Kirlian photography and other techniques have pretty well proven the existence of an energy field around us, one we can see with some practice and the right mind set. I have seen enough auras to believe I could do it most of the time if I so chose. Much more is to be learned about this energy field around our bodies.

Is mind over matter real? I think so, therefore in my reality it is so. I have a mechanical engineering background, yet the pendulum moved in ways I cannot explain. Other experiences I had along my five year journey have further convinced me that the mind is very powerful indeed when it comes to moving or changing objects.

Do I believe in miracles? Yes, because they have happened to me. Creative visualization to get what you want works in our everyday world, and is easy to try yourself. My own evolution towards living in the present, achieving wisdom, and experiencing serenity is in itself miraculous, considering my compulsive, judgmental, anxiety ridden past. Anything is possible if your desire and imagination are strong enough.

Is there life after death? Unequivocally, yes. Too much evidence has come my way to believe any differently. That energy field we see as an aura does not go away, for energy doesn't die. It transforms, much as ice turns to water, then to gas when heated enough. Our technology is taking us closer to proving this continuation of life away from the physical body. Even without such machinery, there exist today many ways you can prove to yourself that physical death need not be feared.

Do we go to heaven or hell when we leave physical form? I think we go where we believe we will go, as I am now convinced we co-create, along with God and other people, much of our reality with our minds. Our minds do not cease after death, thus they continue to co-create another living reality after physical death.

Are we eternal? Who knows? If you are truly living in the present moment, then now is all there is. There may be an infinite number of nows for all of us, but since all we have is now, let's enjoy it to the fullest. Until eternity ends I'm going to concentrate on enjoying the present.

Is there a God? There has to be, though I believe we have little conception yet of that awesome energy called God, which I believe to be love. But please, define God yourself, in your own way, as I have in mine. One of the mistakes I made in the past was to let others define reality for me, instead of making my own decisions.

Do I expect you to believe all of this? No, as I am in the process of giving up the need to be right. Your world is as you see it, and that is fine with me. Harricharan says "What you think of me is none of my business." That goes for my experiences, too: take what you like and leave the rest.

I don't expect many of you to follow a path similar to mine; after all, mine has been a bit unconventional. If some of what happened to me on my journey is of interest to you, try it for yourself, then you decide. This book is not intended to convince anyone about anything, except that *you can survive, learn and grow after an overwhelming loss changes your world.*

Throughout my recovery , I too often played my old tapes for coping with life, tapes that denied my emotions and pretended that all was fine. But those tapes couldn't last under the steady onslaught of hurt, and the pain seeped through my carefully constructed emotional dam.

My new ways of coping, my new behavior tapes, allow me to risk sharing my feelings more

153

honestly with others. Those emotions aren't as likely to be submerged any longer.

In fact, I believe losing Brenda and eventually Sandy opened the floodgates of my long-stored feelings, greatly increasing the intensity and duration of those emotions. The grief over my losses may have lasted longer than for more emotionally expressive people, since my codependent nature had not allowed me to release pent-up feelings over the years.

Loss is a part of life. Whether the loss is small, such as losing the keys to the car, or enormous, such as the death of a loved one, grief will be present. The shock, denial, anger and depression will probably occur to some degree, along with other emotions such as fear, guilt, hurt, self-pity, and anxiety. I think we can lessen the impact of such powerful emotions by being prepared for them.

If losses accumulate inside without travelling along the grieving path towards acceptance of the loss, I believe the stress can become enormous. Possibly, losses not processed through grieving may have contributed heavily to Brenda's suicide.

Her son chose to live with his father, and continued to have trouble with the authorities. Her father had died several years before, but in retrospect I don't remember her crying much or showing many of the symptoms of deep grief. She perceived her youth as fading, and had many health problems. She had been injured by the friend falling on her, and her home had been violated by the house sitter. All were losses to her.

She believed I, too, might become a loss if we divorced. She couldn't find work that satisfied her for very long, thus she had to deal frequently with the loss of her job. She also feared she might lose her mind, as her grandmother had years before.

The cumulative effect of these real and imagined losses, whether big or small, may have built an unbearable pressure inside her, which might have been relieved by openly grieving. Perhaps the pressure became intolerable when electroshock treatment was withheld, which may have contributed to her last loss, that of hope.

Had Brenda been able to grieve, to cry, to rage, and to process the feelings of loss, she may not have felt pushed irrevocably away from life; she might have recognized her losses and grieved them. She, like so many of us, had never learned about dealing with losses, about grieving.

It is my hope and desire that courses will be developed for all of us, hopefully at an early age, to deal with loss and the grief that follows. The Therese Rando book, Grieving, or The Grief Recovery Handbook by John James and Frank Cherry, would make excellent texts for such courses. Perhaps one of the reasons our society has become an angry one in many ways results, in part, from unexpressed anger and other emotions that have not been processed through grief work.

Many questions and thoughts about Brenda remain with me. I've mentioned above one possible contribution to the despair that brought her death, but there are other possibilities. For one, the manic-depression and alcohol and drug problems most definitely had a devastating effect, but there were reasons she turned to them. Since manic depressives seem to suffer from chronic insomnia, the pills and alcohol may have given her some sleep, though of poor quality.

But the mix of chemicals in her body also contributed greatly to her ill health and outlook. She was caught between needing the alcohol, as the only drug she could find to relieve the agony of her condition, and the knowledge that the alcohol and pills were poisoning her system.

Long before the manic depression surfaced, Brenda suffered from a sizeable list of allergies. Those alone often drove her wild. She feared another bee sting, for the doctors said another sting might kill her. Her dry skin and the eczema in her hair kept her scratching constantly. There is some evidence now that allergies do contribute to suicide.

She rarely found a comfortable position for sleep because of her chronically sore back. There were days when she could barely get out of bed due to her apparent rheumatoid arthritis. Her legs would frequently cramp painfully. I believe the allergies and aches alone might cause someone to want to escape their body.

Brenda was once diagnosed as borderline hypo-glycemic and her mother was a diabetic. She also suffered some female problems that required surgery and treatment, including chronic yeast infections and PMS. With all this going on in her body, who can imagine what agony she really felt?

Her many ailments and addictions go a long way towards a traditional explanation of why she killed herself, but I'll never really know why. Her determination to die would probably have defied most rescue attempts. In fact, there are other more metaphysical explanations possible. She may have suffered from spirit possession on occasion, particularly when drunk.

Sixty years ago, medical doctor E.C. Wickland and his wife, who was a psychic, conducted experiments using electroshock therapy to verify results. In his book 30 Years Among the Dead he cites several cases of suicidal individuals being cured after being clinically shock treated.

His contention was that the invading spirit had killed itself in its own life, only to find it was still "alive" in another time dimension. This spirit would then invade the patient, who typically was under the influence of alcohol or drugs, and then try to kill itself again, not realizing it was inhabiting someone else's body.

This potential explanation could fit Brenda. She had many psychic experiences, and her personality shifts and suicidal behavior, when under the influence of drugs and alcohol, were dramatically different from her normal behavior. The night she died, my neighbor Martha saw her as she walked into our house from the front porch swing. She said her eyes looked like they were on fire, as if she was possessed, a look I had seen myself many times.

On a more spiritual level, perhaps a higher power knew that in order for my life and the lives of many others to change, Brenda must leave us. I don't pretend to understand the workings of the many universes surrounding us or the mind and will of God, but I do accept that I probably would not have made the changes in myself if Brenda had not died. She may have left us so some of us would be forced to learn, grow, and change.

Do I condemn Brenda for killing herself? No, because I didn't walk in her shoes. If reincarnation and karma are a reality, then she came into this life to deal with her addictions, but wasn't yet strong enough to conquer them. Perhaps she tried to take on too much. Besides, it was her life, not mine and not anyone else's.

Does her spirit still exist? I believe so, and I think occasionally she touches into my life to see how I'm doing. In fact, I and several psychics sensed her around me frequently as I finished this book.

Will she reincarnate? I suppose so, though I don't worry much about when or where. There was a time I believed she had planned to come back, but decided to continue lessons on the other side for awhile before returning to our physical plane for more lessons here.

Do I miss her? Of course, but not as painfully as in the beginning. I see her more as she really was, someone I once loved but often had difficulty liking because of her addictions, afflictions and behavior. In all honesty, though, I would give a great deal to have her back, if that were possible, particularly with what I know now.

Time has worked its magic with me, though, and five years later I believe I'm fairly well healed from the deep psychic wound brought on by her death. I know in my heart someday we will meet again somewhere.

I hope your own path can include a new spirituality for you as mine did. It has helped me learn to deal with death as the end of a phase in this eternal life. Find for yourself teachers, orthodox or otherwise, that can help you chart your own destiny from now on. Learn and grow as best you can from your experiences, as I am trying to. Look for a new center for your own life.

I said at the beginning of this book that I lost Brenda, the center of my life, in July 1984. A part of me will always love and miss her, but I have found a different center for my life now, one that can never go away.

It allows me to be emotional, more clearly focussed, and truly happier. The new center, which is not new at all, allows me to love others more fully. My goal in life is to become more like that center, which has always been and will always be. That spiritual center of my life is the part of me that is part of God.

Chapter 12

What Worked for Me

I've assembled here some ways of coping with severe loss that I learned along my path through grief. These may or may not work for you; they definitely worked for me.

I can't tell you how to grieve or how to emerge from that grief. I haven't been where you've been, nor can I go where you're going. You are unique and will heal in your own unique way. Take what you can use of these guidelines, but use them in <u>your own</u> way.

Guidelines are only suggestions, they are not laws to be obeyed or broken. Choosing to ignore guidelines won't make you a bad person, nor will your recovery necessarily be more difficult. Guidelines may point the way for you, but only if they feel right to you. The choice to follow or not follow them is yours.

Though I wrote these guidelines on my own, many are mentioned by Iris Bolton and others in their literature. They helped and are helping me keep some balance as I continue to heal, learn and grow. Here they are:

- Let your emotions flow as often as possible, particularly during deep grief episodes. I believe that getting in touch with our emotions, even the painful ones, is a major reason we are living on this earth. Blockages to your expressing emotions have been blown away by the enormity of your loss. I believe we are striving towards that highest emotion called love (or God), but can't get there without experiencing all the other emotions along the way. This period of intense sorrow will, if you will let it, lead you through many emotions towards that goal of universal love.

- Allow the new people appearing in your life to help. They are there for a reason, whether you believe they are just chance meetings, or are sent from God, or were known by you in past lives. Welcome them to your new reality. You may find much more support from them than from old friends and family. Those old friends and family usually knew you and your lost loved one as a couple and probably know some of your past weaknesses. Without meaning to, they may play on those weaknesses, whereas new people are more inclined to accept you just as you are now. When you are stronger, you may be better able to deal more effectively with those who used to be close to you, and could be again.

- Build yourself a support system of as many people as you can. If a grief group such as Survivors of Suicide is nearby, go to their meetings. My Al-Anon group was also wonderfully supportive in those early days of loss. Having sensitive other people at hand can give hope in the darkest moments. Don't trap yourself into "holding up well" all the time; it takes too much energy.

- Use your support system as you need it. If someone in that group of supporters doesn't have time to listen, turn to another. You may find that after awhile you're able to support them, too. They may be in need of help and your knowledge shared with them may make you feel more worthwhile. Sharing healing energy with others was part of my learning and growing. Besides, it just feels good to be loving and be loved by others for just who you are right now.

- Give yourself permission to need a professional counselor for now. A good counselor familiar with the process of grieving can be part of your support team. Look for a caring psychotherapist, social worker, psychologist, psychiatrist, family doctor, minister, hypnotherapist, etc. In my own case, I found compassionate psychic healers helped me the most, since they apparently receive assistance from unseen sources. They could zero in on my problems faster than traditional counselors.

- Heal at your own speed. No good counselor, book, or any other source besides yourself can tell you when to feel. Therefore, there is no time limit on your grief. Most people will expect you to be over your loss much sooner than what may be appropriate for you. In my own case, I still have remnants of grief after five years, though I began to feel more "normal" after around two years.

- Give time a chance to help you recover. You have been dealt an enormous psychic wound. For that hurt to heal properly, give it regular doses of time. Don't pretend to be recovered until you <u>feel</u> recovered.

- Don't try to get perfect, just get better. So many of us have been trained to be perfect, when in reality we are learning and growing bit by bit. Too often, we are attached to a need to be right, thus thinking perhaps we are perfect. Learning takes time, it takes mistakes, and it takes that necessary forgiveness of yourself and others for the inevitable errors we learners make. True perfection may be reserved for a higher power such as God, though perhaps even God would be bored if perfect.

- Go ahead and cry, whenever you feel like it. Crying is the fastest relief I know of to purge sorrow from your heart. Crying wasn't easy for me, so occasionally when I felt a need to, I would play old songs or look at pictures that brought back memories. Holding in the tears may delay your healing from the deep psychic wound you've received. When the body is cut, blood flows to cleanse the wound. So do tears cleanse the emotional wound.

- Self-pity for awhile is normal. Bathe in feeling sorry for yourself until you grow tired of it. Hopefully, you will come to a time when you recognize that self-pity is not healing you. Then you can become motivated toward truly living again instead of cursing your fate. You need not be a victim unless you choose to be one.

- Take care of yourself. Allow more time to do what has to be done, for depression will slow you down. It takes a lot of energy to grieve, so be sure to eat well, even if often you don't feel hungry. Extra vitamin supplements for stress may help. Long walks calmed my frazzled nerves. Take medications if you must, but do so only with your doctor's advice. Get a massage or chiropractic adjustment, if aches and pains contribute to your sleeplessness.

- Soothing music may help you relax. I often soak in a hot tub with very soft music playing to calm me down. The right music for you will become apparent if you try several different types.

- Find hobbies that make you feel better. I gardened, read books, watched TV, and worked with the pendulum. Whether old recreations or new, hobbies keep us living in the present moment and often provide hours of relatively peaceful diversion.

- Be honest with your feelings. Tell others how you feel. Feelings are neither right nor wrong, they just are. Try not to add to your large dose of guilt by ignoring the intense emotions you'll be experiencing for awhile. You'll be pleasantly surprised at the compassion most people will show when you share your true feelings with them. For those who don't show the compassion you expect, try to see that they are being who they choose to be, for whatever reason.

- Go easy on yourself. Avoid any major decisions for as long as possible, preferably at least one year, until you are stronger and more balanced. You are already under enough stress. Your loss has probably knocked you far away from being centered, so try to put some time between the loss and big changes in your residence, job, religion, etc. You'll probably make a better decision after at least some months have passed.

- Follow your hunches, intuition, gut feelings, or whatever you call your sixth sense. I believe we all have abilities in this area that need development and practice, as we would practice a golf swing, bidding in bridge, flying an airplane or running a business. The more you use this wonderful intuitive talent, the more accurate and reliable it will become. You may find, as I did, that learning to use this ability will in some small way compensate for your loss.

- Talk to your lost loved one, or your guardian angel, guide, God or imaginary friends. You may feel foolish doing so, however, you don't have to talk out loud. The act of using your imagination and releasing some of your emotions this way may help you heal. If such spirits are in fact real, they may send you messages back (perhaps as intuition or in dreams) that could support you in your time of need.

- Become more comfortable with the reality of physical death. My friend was right when he said "What is, is." A belief in the survival of the soul helps, though that is not essential to accepting the fact that we will all die. When the reality of death sank into me, I became more determined to live my life more fully, to learn as much as I could before my time comes. I

167

now look at that time for me as a transition to a new life somewhere else, rather than the oblivion some would have us believe.

- Try to live more in the present. It's difficult at first, because deep grief pushes you back to past memories and brings up fear of the future without your lost loved one. I found that my gradual evolution towards being happy with the present moment has made my life much more pleasant. The future seems less threatening when "right now" is fine, even if right now is painful. Both the past and the future are just thoughts now, so try to control those thoughts by being more aware of what is happening right this instant.

- "One day at a time" helps focus on the present moment. It helps set the goal of getting through another day. Soon, those days become weeks, months and years, when long range goals can have meaning again. If a whole day is too much at first, start with 60 seconds or an hour or this morning, until the days become more manageable. The determination to take life in little pieces may make each of those pieces easier to live.

- Believe that you do the best you can with what you knew at the time, or with where you are at the time. I have felt this way since I was very young. This belief may make it easier for you to forgive yourself for what you didn't do in the past because you didn't know then what you know now. If you did the best you could with the knowledge you had in the past, why stop now? You may find this approach will help you live more completely in the present.

- Get good and mad once in awhile. At some point, you'll probably be very angry at the one you lost, or with old friends who don't seem to understand, or strangers who say the wrong thing, or God, or even yourself. Anger is a legitimate emotion and you have a right to your feelings. Expressing anger is part of your healing, as well as part of your growth. I believe an occasionally angry person is becoming a healthy person by expressing the anger. If you choose not to express your anger, it may reappear much later in a tirade directed at an innocent target, or worse, within your own body as an illness.

- It's all right to say "I don't know." We'll never know exactly why our loved one chose to die. In fact, as we learn and grow, what we don't know becomes more obvious. Even when others ask us how we're doing, aren't there a lot of times we just don't know? You may want to permit yourself to say so. Being willing not to know may take some of the pressure off your already overburdened self.

- You aren't responsible for other people's actions or feelings. The ultimate decision on what to do with your life rests with you, as it does with all of us. They are your feelings, your actions. Doesn't everyone else have the same right and responsibility? One of my greatest lessons, from my tragedy, was learning to let go of my codependent need to be responsible for someone else's behavior. Honor the right of others to choose their own destiny, as you must decide yours.

- Your life is different now. It's never going to be the same, so perhaps embracing some of the differentness may lessen the fears of your changed life. No matter how hard we try to build security into our lives, something always seems to change. Becoming more comfortable with the reality of change has made me more accepting of the constant ebb and flow that is life.

- Meditation does work. If you feel comfortable doing so, take at least 15 minutes a day, preferably in the early morning or late at night, to deliberately relax alone and idle your mind motor. Soft music and guided meditation tapes helped me do so. You can also treat yourself to this healing way of reflection while doing needlepoint, ironing, walking, or, in my case, bathing or mowing the lawn. Set your mind to neutral and you'll be surprised at the messages that become apparent. I've heard it said that praying is asking and meditation is listening.

- Use your time alone to peel back layered memories. Whether memories of this life or others, you may find insight into who you really are and why you do what you do. In my case, the past lives research I began about six months after Brenda died not only gave me valuable information about me and my relationships, it became a pastime that filled some of my lonely months.

- Release some of your stored emotions. Sometimes feelings such as anger, fear, anxiety and hate show up in the body as backstrain, headaches or muscle tension. These blocked feelings may have been there for years. Often counselors, chiropractors, massage therapists, or psychic healers can help you release these stored emotions. Letting go of these emotional blockages might lessen your pain and may assist your learning and growing.

- Pain is part of life. Your mother went through real pain during your birth, didn't she? Pain can be used to look for causes, and looking for causes often promotes growth. If the pain has been caused by hurt, as is so often the case in suicide, it takes time to heal. It will ease as time passes. You don't have to like the pain, but you can use it to learn.

- Fear is normal after severe loss. Acknowledge and identify your fears if you can, for recognizing a problem is the first step towards curing it. This may be the single greatest challenge for you, that of lessening your fears. I found that letting go of the past and living more in the present alleviated many of my own fears.

- Take charge of your guilt if you can. Some say guilt is anger you don't feel you have the right to express. Whatever it is, though, it is your guilt, to do with as you see fit. No one else owns it. Feel it when you must, but be wary of those who feed it. Remorse or sadness is not the same as guilt. You'll feel a legitimate sadness about your loss, but you need not feel guilty unless you choose to. Humans have apparently invented guilt; animals don't seem to know the meaning of the word.

- Use breathing techniques to ease your stress. Have you ever watched a dog take a deep breath when it wants to relax? The animals we share the planet with can teach us much, if we take the time to watch them. They know instinctively how to deal with stress. There are many breathing techniques you can learn. I found the simplest is to take a deep breath, hold it for a few seconds, blow out through the mouth and repeat a couple of times. The oxygen boost to the blood from deep breathing seems to make me feel better right away.

- Commitment may be difficult for some time. I found it hard to commit to anyone or anything outside myself for a long time. Making yourself the center of your own existence for awhile may make it easier to commit to others after more time has passed. Love yourself as much as you can, so you'll be able to love others more later. Healing your own heart may allow you to be more giving towards and forgiving of others.

- Your ability to feel and care may be inhibited for awhile. Some of the inhibition in the beginning may be from shock, some may be from fear of losing again, and some from early training. You may have to work at risking feelings for others once more, since you've been hurt so badly. Many of my own loving feelings were frozen for years after my wife's death because I didn't want more hurt.

- Be patient with yourself as you attempt social contacts again. In my case I had to learn to date once more, and even going out with friends occasionally was difficult, at first. If your loss leads to dating someday, be wary of looking for a replacement for your lost loved one. Try to accept people as they are rather than as you would have them be.

- Flaws in others may mirror flaws in ourselves. When you get upset about the way someone else behaves, look inside to see if they reflect something in yourself you might want to change. You can change if you choose; sometimes we have to see ourselves in others to realize we need to change something within us.

- Judging the reactions and behavior of others may block your recovery and growth. They are doing the best they can with their lives, just as you are. If others occasionally rub you the wrong way, you may want to wait awhile before deciding you don't want them in your life anymore. However, do be discerning in who you choose to trust, for you are very vulnerable right now.

- Take time now to think about your life, what it has meant and what it can mean. You will have periods of intense loneliness, but some of those times alone can be turned into a healthy review of who you are and where you stand. Though sometimes painfully slow and filled with confusion, doubt, anxiety, worry, fear and guilt, these solitary times of looking within may begin to show you the many wonderful sides of that complex spirit that is the real you.

- Forgiving is a wonderful healing experience. When you feel you can, forgive the one you lost for leaving you, forgive those who seem insensitive to your feelings, and most important of all, forgive yourself for being human. You will probably do and say things while recovering from deep grief that you'll be sorry for later. That is normal and certainly forgivable. Forgiveness frees you to live again, instead of just existing.

- Give yourself permission to feel good about you, if possible. You might even do something frivolous. Though you may feel foolish or guilty for doing so, your life is moving on. Remembering frivolous times from the past may encourage you to try it again, perhaps adding a new carefree memory in your life.

- People aren't right or wrong, they just are. They aren't better than, nor less than, just different than you are. You can't change them, they must change themselves. If their choice of behavior isn't comfortable for you, put what distance you can between yourself and them. They, too, are learning in their own way, but their way may not be beneficial to you for awhile.

- You really don't own anything on this earth. If you think you own your house, what if the government decides a highway should go through your land? Fire can strike the house, or circumstances can cause the bank to foreclose. Likewise, do we own our bodies, or are they just rented for the span of this life on earth? Believing we rent all we consider possessions has given me greater peace of mind, since I'm no longer as attached as I was to my beliefs, or items, or to people, as I used to be. I still value my body, my possessions, and the people in my life, but I don't own them, nor do they own me.

- Watch for a return of your sense of humor. Laughter, particularly at yourself, is a sure sign you are getting better. Along with the tears, laughter is an extraordinarily powerful healer. I now use my sense of humor as a barometer to indicate whether I'm stressed out or not.

- Believe what your experiences tell you. I was told "Experience is what you get when you don't get what you want." Allow those experiences to teach you, and perhaps you won't have to repeat some lessons again. You will learn best from your own experiences, not someone else's.

- As you walk your lonely road back to a more normal life, remember some of what your lost loved one taught you. They have left you changed by their presence, changes that might not have occurred had they not been part of your life. Cherish the stamp they have imprinted on you. Thank them in your own way when you have an experience you might not have recognized if they hadn't opened your eyes to it. Try to make their death help you focus on the forced rebirth of your own life.

- Your world hasn't ended. Though it may often seem so, what has ended is your world together. It is the start of your new world. What you decide to make of your new world is your choice. You can choose to learn and grow from the tragedy. Remember the story of the man who pitied his shoeless condition until he saw a man who had no feet? Take your own feet and walk through this rain in your life. You are not walking as alone as you may sometimes think. Your anguish is real, but so is the strength of your magnificent mind, body and spirit.

- When one door closes, another opens. New beginnings come from old endings. Grow as you can, learn as you will. You may be afraid, as I was, to walk through the new door in your life. I was literally kicked through that door, but I'm a different and better person now. I've found a new life on the other side of my closed door.

- There may be treasures (or gifts) from your loss that seem impossible now. Perhaps sooner than you think you will find one of them. And, like a treasure hunt, you might find more of these gifts, these lessons, this learning and growing that seems so painful now. My gifts included my more mature friendship with my mother, my insight into my own problems, my belief in eternal life, and my spirituality.

- Hope is waiting for you to find it. The old saying is right - all things do pass, including this loss. I didn't lose hope because I had the message to learn and grow from my wife's suicide. Even when the days are darkest, there is always the hope for a better tomorrow.

- The only way to recover from this great loss is your way. Not my way, or your best friend's way, or your counselor's. Your own special, unique way, at your own pace. No one has ever, or will ever, walk in your shoes. Only you know what is best for you. Decide what that is and do it. Take from others what works for you and leave the rest. You can and will survive and grow from this, but it must be done your way.

Bibliography

Codependence

Beattie, Melody. *Codependent No More.* New York: Harper/Hazelden, 1987.

Larsen, Ernie. *Stage II Relationships - Love Beyond Addiction.* New York: Harper & Row, 1987.

Norwood, Robin. *Women Who Love Too Much.* Los Angeles: Jeremy P. Tarcher, 1985.

Schaef, Anne Wilson. *When Society Becomes an Addict.* New York: Harper & Row, 1987.

Whitfield, Charles L., M.D. *Healing the Child Within.* Deerfield Bch, FL: Health Comm., 1987.

Woititz, Janet G., Ed. D. *Struggle for Intimacy.* Deerfield Beach, FL: Health Comm., 1985.

Death & Dying

Kubler-Ross, Elisabeth, M.D. *Questions and Answers on Death and Dying.* N.Y.: Macmillan, 1974.

Levine, Stephen. *Who Dies?* New York: Anchor Press/Doubleday, 1982.

White, John. *A Practical Guide to Death & Dying.* Wheaton, IL: Quest Books, 1980.

Grieving

Berkus, Rusty. *To Heal Again.* Encino, CA: Red Rose Press, 1984.

Bolton, Iris. *My Son... My Son....* Atlanta, GA: Bolton Press, 1983.

Elmer, Lon. *Why Her Why Now.* Seattle, WA: Signal Elm Press, 1987.

Grollman, Earl. *Living When a Loved One Has Died.* Boston: Beacon Press, 1977.

James, John W. & Cherry, Frank. *The Grief Recovery Handbook.* New York: Harper & Row, 1988.

Kushner, Harold S. *When Bad Things Happen to Good People.* New York: Avon Books, 1981.

Rando, Therese A., Ph.D. *Grieving: How to Go on Living When Someone You Love Dies.* Lexington, MA: Lexington Books, 1988.

Tatelbaum, Judy. *The Courage to Grieve.* New York: Harper & Row, 1980.

Life After Death

Lenz, Frederick, Ph.D. *Life Times.* New York: Fawcett Crest, 1979.

Martin, Joel & Romanowski, Patricia. *We Don't Die.* New York: Berkley Books, 1988.

Meek, George W. *After We die, What Then?* Franklin, NC: Metascience Publications, 1980.

Montgomery, Ruth. *A World Beyond.* New York: Fawcett Crest, 1971.

Moody, Raymond A., Jr. M.D. *Life After Life.* New York: Bantam, 1975.

Osis, Karlis, Ph.D. & Haraldsson, Erlendur, Ph.D. *At the Hour of Death.* N.Y.: Discus/Avon, 1977.

Rawlings, Maurice, M.D. *Beyond Death's Door.* New York: Bantam Books, 1978.

Sherman, Harold. *The Dead Are Alive.* New York: Fawcett Gold Medal, 1981.

Steiger, Brad. *The World Beyond Death.* Norfolk, VA: The Donning Company, 1982.

Wickland, E. C., M.D. *30 Years Among the Dead.* Newcastle Publishing, 1927.

Past Lives

Fiore, Dr. Edith. *You Have Been Here Before.* New York: Ballantine Books, 1978.

Langley, Noel. *Edgar Cayce on Reincarnation.* New York: Warner Books, 1967.

Montgomery, Ruth. *The World Before.* New York: Fawcett/Crest, 1976.

Stearn, Jess. *Soulmates.* New York: Bantam, 1984.

Steiger, Brad. *You Will Live Again.* New York: Dell/Confucian, 1978.

Sutphen, Dick. *You Were Born Again to Be Together.* New York: Pocket Books, 1976.

Wambach, Helen, Ph.D. *Life Before Life.* New York: Bantam Books, 1979.

Personal Development

Bach, Richard. *The Bridge Across Forever.* New York: William Morrow, 1984.

Buscaglia, Leo. *Loving Each Other.* Thorofare, NJ: SLACK, 1984.

Dyer, Dr. Wayne W. *The Sky's the Limit.* New York: Simon & Schuster, 1980.

Kraft-Macoy, Liah. *30 Days to Happiness.* Walpole, NH: Stillpoint, 1987.

Peck, M. Scott., M.D. *The Road Less Travelled.* New York: Simon & Schuster, 1978.

Roman, Sanaya. *Living with Joy.* Tiburon, CA: H. J. Kramer, 1986.

Smith, Manuel J., Ph.D. *When I Say No, I Feel Guilty.* New York: Bantam Books, 1975.

Steiger, Brad & Steiger, Francie. *The Star People.* New York: Berkley Books, 1981.

Viorst, Judith. *Necessary Losses.* New York: Simon & Schuster, 1986.

Viscott, David, M D. *The Language of Feelings.* New York: Pocket Books, 1976.

Psychic & Spiritual Growth

Gawain, Shakti. *Living In The Light.* San Rafael, CA: Whatever Publishing, 1986.

Harricharan, John. *When You Can Walk on Water, Take the Boat.* Marietta, GA: New World Publishing, 1986.

James, Eliott. *Attaining The Mastership.* Atlanta, GA: Dhamma Books, 1988.

Lazaris. *The Sacred Journey: You and Your Higher Self.* Beverly Hills, CA: Concept: Synergy Publishing, 1987.

MacLaine, Shirley. *Out on a Limb.* New York: Bantam Books, 1983.

Roberts, Jane. *Seth Speaks.* New York: Bantam Books, 1972.

Woodrew, Greta. *Memories of Tomorrow.* New York: Dolphin/Doubleday, 1988.

Yarbro, Chelsea Quinn. *Messages from Michael.* New York: Berkley Books, 1979.

About the Author

Jack Clarke is just another man striving for peace and happiness in an often confusing world. He conducts regular sales training courses titled "Listen for the Order" and is a licensed real estate broker. He writes music and book reviews, plus articles, for <u>Body, Mind & Spirit</u> magazine and other publications. He created two inspirational prints about human development, which have been distributed around the world and about which he speaks to groups. He conducts a Survivors of Suicide support group and is planning a series of workshops on dealing with loss, titled "Recovery from Change."

Born in a suburb of New York City, raised near Chicago, and a resident of the Atlanta area for 26 years, he attended Cornell University. He graduated from the University of Wisconsin - Madison with a degree in finance (after three years of mechanical engineering) and did graduate work at Georgia State University.

A decorated infantry officer during the early Vietnam era, he went on to build award winning careers in computer sales and management while also operating his real estate business. He served voluntarily for a time as vice president and board member of an Atlanta non-profit organization that promotes personal growth, acting as reviews editor, distribution manager, and performing other functions for their newspaper and special events.

He is an avid gardener, specializing in roses, listens to and collects music, reads when he can and loves to travel, particularly in Australia. He is actively trying to get in touch with his right brain, cure his addiction to fixing people, establish a healthy committed relationship, maintain his sense of humor, and return to a childlike view of the universe.